Children's Books of International Interest

Third Edition

Barbara Elleman
Editor

International Relations Committee
Association for Library Service to Children
American Library Association

American Library Association
Chicago 1984

Subcommittee of the
INTERNATIONAL RELATIONS COMMITTEE
Association for Library Service to Children

Pat Bakula, Youth Librarian, Maude Shunk Library, Menomonee
Falls, Wisconsin

Ginny Moore Kruse, Director, Cooperative Children's Book Cen-
ter, Madison, Wisconsin

Micki Nevett, Children's and Young Adult Consultant, Mohawk
Valley Library System, Schenectady, New York

Mary Lou White, Professor, Wright State University, Dayton,
Ohio

Consultant, Barbara Elleman, Editor, Children's Books, *Booklist*,
American Library Association

Library of Congress Cataloging in Publication Data
Main entry under title:

Children's books of international interest.

   Rev. ed. of: Children's books of international in-
terest / Virginia Haviland, editor. 2nd ed. 1978.
   Includes index.
   1. Children's literature, American—Bibliography.
I. Elleman, Barbara. II. Haviland, Virginia, 1911-
Children's books of international interest. III. ALSC
International Relations Committee. IV. Title.
Z1037.C5436 1984 [PN1009.A1] 011'.62 84-20336
ISBN 0-8389-3314-9

Contents

Preface

In the preface to the second edition, Virginia Haviland speaks thoughtfully about the need to help promote international understanding through children's books; six years later these remarks still stand well and are retained for readers' continued perusal. She deftly traces the role of the Association for Library Service to Children in the international arena and provides solid guidelines for the selection of books of international interest.

In this edition, however, one area of emphasis has changed. Translation and foreign-language rights, previously regarded as a major reason for the bibliography, are now commonly negotiated at the annual Bologna and Frankfurt Book Fairs. With this change in mind, the committee shifted its focus to collection development and individual reading guidance in the hope that teachers and librarians both here and abroad will use the bibliography to help children realize their place as world citizens.

In making selections from the 1978 edition of *Children's Books of International Interest* and the subsequent annual lists prepared by the International Relations Committee of the Association for Library Service to Children, the committee kept specific criteria in mind. Guidelines required that the titles be of high-quality, appeal to children, and either incorporate universal themes or depict the American way of life. Titles selected represent both books that children the world over can relate to through character, plot, and theme and books that can provide an introduction to the United States through a variety of concepts, ideas, and happenings. All titles listed are currently in print at time of publication of this edition. Although fluctuating prices are difficult to verify, those used here reflect the trade price listed in the 1983–84 *Children's Books in Print* and will give book buyers an approximation of the book's cost. More than 215 new main entries have been added and 136 titles from the second edition have been retained.

It is the committee's hope that this new edition will be useful to people in other countries as well as to those in the United States who are making this world a better place for children to live and grow.

Barbara Elleman
Editor

Preface to the
Second Edition

Among the aims of UNESCO for International Book Year was the improvement of the production and distribution of books through international exchange. This has been a motivating ideal, too, for children's librarians organized within the American Library Association. Since 1955, a decade and a half preceding the designation of 1972 as International Book Year, the Association for Library Service to Children (formerly the Children's Services Division) of the American Library Association, through its International Relations Committee, has expressed in a special bibliographic series its belief in the value of the international exchange of children's books. This has been the purpose of the succession of annual lists entitled *U.S.A. Children's Books of International Interest* (previously entitled *Books Recommended for Translation*). Over the years these lists have been made available by mail and at international congresses—the International Federation of Library Associations (IFLA) and the International Board on Books for Young People (IBBY)—to librarians, publishers, booksellers, and others seeking to promote the production and distribution of good books internationally.

The role of internationalism in promoting understanding and cooperation is becoming more widely recognized in the world of children's books. The flow of books between countries and copublishing arrangements are being furthered at the Bologna Children's Book Fair as well as at the Frankfurt Book Fair. As recognition is given by means of international and other prizes, notably IBBY's Hans Christian Andersen's biennial medals, awarded since 1956 for the writing and, since 1966, for the illustration of children's books, the necessary exchange of information about good books has been intensified.

The American Library Association considered it significant as an American project for International Book Year in 1972 to take a fresh, retrospective look at the children's books produced in the United States during the past four decades and at its annual lists in order to reevaluate the whole with the support of the test of time, to note those books superseded by later publications, and to take account of changing interests and developments in the world of children.

The initial list issued by the American Library Association in 1955 comprised 100 titles published from 1930 through 1954. Succeeding annual lists contained from twenty to sixty books each which the committee estimated to have both literary value and universality of interest: picture-story books, fiction, folklore, biography, history, science, and other factual books. Longtime classics, except for a few freshly illustrated editions which thus attained a new look, did not appear. A selection of some 700 was made for the first edition of a composite selected list published in 1972.

Five years later with the help of committee members Sybille Jagusch, Amy Kellman, Elizabeth Murphy, Mary Lett Robertson, Deborah Weilerstein, and others on the annual selection committees, and of Margaret N. Coughlan of the Library of Congress, titles still in print from the 1972 composite list and on subsequent annual lists were considered individually. Some separate entries have been eliminated by combining into a single entry companion works by an author. Some titles, overlooked in the year following publication, have been newly listed on the basis of proven importance. Always the choice to retain or add a title has been based on the aim of past committees to present work which is a genuine contribution to literature for children and young people. Questions have been asked abroad about kinds of books sought for republishing. As was considered each year, picture books selected are still "recommended for consideration provided that pictures as well as story can be reproduced. Each of these books is notable because of the unity of text and pictures." The wide range of fiction represented indicates belief in the sustaining strength and universality of creative writing. The smaller proportion of nonfiction that has remained after the sifting reveals the hard fact that informational books in general have a shorter life.

Many reasons support our belief in the importance of compiling this summary list. Our purposes for the annual lists had been strengthened in 1965 by the concern that sent Mildren L. Batchelder of the American Library Association headquarters staff to Europe on a sabbatical leave to study the acceptance of our translated books. There she discovered that books far less than our best much too often found their way to other countries. The information contained in her interviews with librarians, children's book editors, and others in eleven European countries has enabled us to assess the success or lack of success of translated American books—of particular titles and also of kinds of books—and to learn what kinds of books were sought.

The present, reevaluated, stringent winnowing of the earlier selections highlights the scope and variety of American children's books. It also identifies those intrinsically excellent, enriching, and enduring works, both fiction and nonfiction, which are estimated to have interests for the world abroad. For whom? For publishers, obviously—those who have no specific critical channels established to aid them in making selections. And for their translators, who, similarly, wish to study trends and subject matter and produce editions of the best books for their own countries. For those also who disseminate information about American children's literature—specific books and kinds of books— and who are responsible for the building of American collections in foreign-book areas in libraries. We hope this list will be useful to teachers of children's literature in library schools and teacher-training institutions abroad and to librarians and bibliographers in research centers serving interests in foreign books for young readers. For Americans at home, the list may suggest a basis for the selection of gifts and exhibits sent abroad to represent the United States.

The worldwide translation program which expanded during the post-war years has in the late seventies been reduced for economic reasons. But it is hoped that an upswing in prosperity may come to reduce the risks inherent in publishing translations when book purchasing is reduced. It is our wish that creative writing will balance or replace the overwhelming spread of mass-market books over national borders. Popularity is not excluded here; best-loved books are widely represented, particularly those we feel can best aid true education. We believe this list of exemplary titles, appearing in time to recognize the United Nations' International Year of the Child, will support UNESCO's aim to help developing countries recognize the power of the book as an essential for education, cultural enlightenment, and international understanding.

Virginia Haviland
Editor

Picture Books

Aruego, Jose, and Ariane Dewey. **We Hide, You Seek.** Illus. by the authors. Greenwillow. 1979. 36p. $10.95; lib. ed., $10.51. Ages 3–5.

A brick-red rhinoceros bounces through double-page pictures hunting for his friends, who quietly blend into their surroundings. While there are only four lines of text, enjoyment of this amusing romp comes from locating and identifying the partly hidden animals.

Azarian, Mary. **A Farmer's Alphabet.** Illus. by the author. Godine. 1981. 54p. $12.95; paper, $6.95. Ages 4 and older.

Skillful woodcuts depicting everyday life in rural Vermont illustrate each letter of the alphabet. The scenes are rendered in black ink while the letters, upper- and lower-case, appear in red. Originally designed as a series of posters.

Baker, Olaf. **Where the Buffaloes Begin.** Illus. by Stephen Gammell. Warne. 1981. 48p. $8.95. Ages 7–10.

After Little Wolf finds the legendary lake where the

buffaloes begin, he leads the animals on a terrifying journey to save his Sioux people and becomes part of the legend himself. Handsome, muted black-and-white drawings enhance this powerful tale. A Caldecott Honor Book.

Barrett, Judi. **Cloudy with a Chance of Meatballs.** Illus. by Ron Barrett. Atheneum. 1978. 31p. $9.95; paper, $2.95. Ages 6–8.

One day in Chewandswallow, where all the food is supplied from the sky, the weather takes a turn for the worse, burying everything in a surplus of rotting food. The inhabitants, forced to flee to a new land, learn to shop in supermarkets. An outlandish tall tale illustrated with exaggerated line drawings washed in yellows, olives, and reds.

Baylor, Byrd. **The Way to Start a Day.** Illus. by Peter Parnall. Scribner. 1978. 30p. $10.95. Ages 5–8.

The ways in which various civilizations have greeted the sun each morning with songs and gifts are revealed through double-page spreads strikingly designed to incorporate the poetic text and the illustrator's stiletto drawings. Strong use of line and color enforce the outstanding quality. A Caldecott Honor Book by the same team that created **Desert Voices.**

Bemelmans, Ludwig. **Madeline.** Illus. by the author. Viking. 1939. unp. $11.95; paper, $3.50. Ages 4–7.

Here, as in **Madeline's Rescue** (a Caldecott Medal Book) and the succeeding Madeline picture books, the inventive writer-artist follows the little boarding-school girl in delightful situations. The gay pictures—actual scenes of France and London—provide superb backdrops for the rhyming story.

Bozzo, Maxine Zohn. **Toby in the Country, Toby in the**

City. Illus. by Frank Modell. Greenwillow. 1982. 24p. $10.25; lib. ed., $9.84. Ages 5–8.

A boy and a girl, both named Toby, give identical descriptions of their lives in the country and city. Bright watercolor sketches convey the differences in their surroundings.

Brown, Margaret Wise. **Goodnight Moon.** Illus. by Clement Hurd. Harper. 1947. unp. $6.68; lib. ed., $7.89; paper, $2.95. Ages 2–4.

A little rabbit wishes an individual "Goodnight" to each of his toys, pictures, and pieces of clothing in this favorite bedtime story.

Bunting, Eve. **The Happy Funeral.** Illus. by Vo-Dinh Mai. Harper. 1982. 40p. $8.61; lib. ed., $8.89. Ages 5–9.

During her Chinese-American grandfather's funeral, Laura understands that happiness comes at the end of a good life. Black-and-white sketches illuminate the text.

Burton, Virginia Lee. **The Little House.** Illus. by the author. Houghton. 1942. 40p. $10.50; paper, $2.95. Ages 5–8.

A little house that once stood in the countryside is engulfed by an expanding city. The house's happy return to the country, where it can again enjoy the changing season, is depicted in colorful, superbly designed illustrations. A Caldecott Medal Book.

Burton, Virginia Lee. **Mike Mulligan and His Steam Shovel.** Illus. by the author. Houghton. 1939. 48p. $9.95; paper, $3.95. Ages 3–5.

Mike Mulligan proves that his steam shovel, Mary Anne, can still dig as much in a day as a hundred men can do in a week, even if the diesel and electric shovels are getting all the jobs. With full-color illustrations strong in design, this lively picture book has become an established favorite.

Caines, Jeanette Franklin. **Just Us Women.** Illus. by Pat Cummings. Harper. 1982. 32p. $9.13; lib. ed., $9.89. Ages 5–8.

A young black girl and her aunt plan a long auto trip. Soft two-color illustrations complement the story's relaxed, warm atmosphere.

Calhoun, Mary. **Cross-Country Cat.** Illus. by Erick Ingraham. Morrow. 1979. 40p. $9.25; lib. ed., $8.88. Ages 4–7.

When he is accidentally left at the family cabin, a Siamese cat named Henry makes his way down the mountain on a tiny pair of skis before his people finally rescue him. Illustrations in blue-and-brown tones suit Henry and the wintry countryside equally well.

Carrick, Carol. **Two Coyotes.** Illus. by Donald Carrick. Clarion. 1982. 32p. $11.50. Ages 6–10.

Hunger plagues the male coyote and his pregnant mate. Colorful, realistic illustrations dramatize this survival tale of creatures in the wild.

Clifton, Lucille. **My Friend Jacob.** Illus. by Thomas DiGrazia. Dutton. 1980. 32p. $9.95. Ages 6–9.

Eight-year-old Sam and his mentally retarded neighbor Jacob, 17, learn many things from each other. Muted pencil drawings reflect the warmth of a special friendship.

Cohen, Miriam. **Will I Have a Friend?** Illus. by Lillian Hoban. Macmillan. 1967. unp. $9.95; paper, $2.50. Ages 5–7.

A kindergartener's apprehension about finding a friend on the first day of school is the theme of this warmly appealing story.

Cole, Brock. **No More Baths.** Illus. by the author. Doubleday. 1980. unp. $10.95. Ages 6–8.

4

A young girl with a strong affinity for dirt does *not* change her ways after joining the chickens, cat, and pigs in their daily pursuits.

Crews, Donald. **Freight Train.** Illus. by the author. Greenwillow. 1978. 24p. $10.95; lib. ed., $10.51. Ages 2–5.
A simple concept book introduces familiar colors in pictures of a freight train's different cars. Crews conveys the speed of the rushing train with spare details and almost solid blocks of color. A Caldecott Honor Book. Others in this highly visual series by the same artist include **Light** and **Truck.**

Daugherty, James H. **Andy and the Lion.** Illus. by the author. Viking. 1938. 79p. $12.95. Ages 6–9.
Bold, full-page line drawings with yellow wash tell how Andy, who reads and dreams about lions, finally meets one on the way to school. This variation on the "Androcles and the Lion" story is modernized with robust humor.

de Paola, Tomie. **Charlie Needs a Cloak.** Illus. by the author. Prentice-Hall. 1973. unp. $9.95; paper, $3.95. Ages 4–7.
Lively, colorful drawings follow the work of a shepherd as he makes himself a cloak from sheep's wool.

de Paola, Tomie. **Now One Foot, Now the Other.** Illus. by the author. Putnam. 1981. 48p. $8.95; paper, $3.95. Ages 6–9.
When a stroke paralyzes his grandfather, Bobby teaches him to walk by repeating the same words he heard from his grandfather as a young child: "Now one foot, now the other." Muted blue-and-tan drawings complement the text. A similar intergenerational theme is found in the author's **Nana Upstairs, Nana Downstairs.**

Du Bois, William Pène. **Lion.** Illus. by the author. Viking. 1956. 36p. $12.95; paper, $3.95. Ages 5–8.

The story of how Lion came to be "invented" is paired with brilliant illustrations. A Caldecott Honor Book.

Ets, Marie. **Play with Me.** Illus. by the author. Viking. 1955. 32p. $12.95; paper, $3.95. Ages 3–5.

A young girl frightens meadow creatures with her energetic attempts to make friends, but when she sits in silence her animal playmates return. A Caldecott Honor Book.

Feelings, Muriel L. **Jambo Means Hello: Swahili Alphabet Book.** Illus. by Tom Feelings. Dial. 1974. unp. $11.95; lib. ed., $11.89; paper, $3.50. Ages 5–8.

A book outstanding for the rich beauty of its soft-pencil drawings and the simplicity of its text introduces 24 letters used in the Swahili language. A Caldecott Honor Book. **Moja Means One: Swahili Counting Book,** another Caldecott Honor Book illustrated by the same artist, is a similar portrayal of African rural life and culture.

Flack, Marjorie. **Ask Mr. Bear.** Illus. by the author. Macmillan. 1932. 32p. $9.95; paper, $3.50. Ages 3–6.

A tender, repetitive, wholly childlike story about a small boy who, seeking to give his mother a birthday present, discovers the meaning of a "bear hug."

Frasconi, Antonio. **See and Say: A Picture Book in Four Languages** [English, French, Italian & Spanish]. Illus. by the author. Harcourt. 1955. 32p. $6.95; paper, $1.35. Ages 5–8.

Colorful woodcuts show simple objects with the name of each given in the four languages.

Freeman, Don. **Corduroy.** Illus. by the author. Viking. 1967. 32p. $9.95; paper, $3.50. Ages 4–8.

Corduroy, an appealing toy shop teddy bear whose green corduroy overalls have one button missing, waits for someone to buy him and take him home in this amusing, satisfying tale.

Gág, Wanda. **Millions of Cats.** Illus. by the author. Coward. 1928. 32p. $7.95; lib. ed., $6.99. Ages 4–8.

A very old man and a very old woman search for one little cat but find themselves with "millions and billions and trillions of cats." A favorite story with a folkloric quality and delightfully droll black-and-white drawings. The author-artist's **Snippy and Snappy** (about two field mice), **Nothing at All** (a puppy), and **The Funny Thing** (an animal?) are also distinctively designed picture-book nonsense stories.

Gardner, Beau. **Turn About, Think About, Look About Book.** Illus. by the author. Lothrop. 1980. 32p. $9.95; lib. ed., $9.95. Ages 6 and older.

In just 14 pages of illustrations, Gardner creates 56 different neon-colored designs. Discovery leads to delight as viewers turn the book upside down and on its sides to see each new perspective.

Ginsburg, Mirra. **Across the Stream.** Based on a verse by Daniil Kharam. Illus. by Nancy Tafuri. Greenwillow. 1982. 23p. $10.25; lib. ed., $9.84. Ages 2–4.

Large, bright paintings and a brief text show how a hen and her chicks cleverly escape from a fox.

Ginsburg, Mirra. **Good Morning, Chick.** Adapted from a story by Kornei Chukovsky. Illus. by Byron Barton. Greenwillow. 1980. unp. $10.95; lib. ed., $10.51. Ages 3–5.

Vivid color, simple forms, and a brief, repetitive text are used to tell the story of a chick's first barnyard experiences.

Greenfield, Eloise. **Grandmama's Joy.** Illus. by Carol Byard. Philomel. 1980. unp. $8.95; lib. ed., $8.99. Ages 6–9.
Despondent over an upcoming move, Grandmother finally is cheered by the reminder that her "joy"—her granddaughter Rondy—will still be with her. Byard's soft brown drawings mesh superbly with the text.

Gundersheimer, Karen. **Happy Winter.** Illus. by the author. Harper. 1982. 40p. $9.57; lib. ed., $9.89. Ages 4–8.
Two little sisters find everyday activities made special by a snowy day. The rhymed text is illustrated with action-filled bright vignettes.

Hall, Donald. **The Ox-Cart Man.** Illus. by Barbara Cooney. Viking. 1979. 40p. $12.95; paper, $3.95. Ages 5–8.
A nineteenth-century New England farmer takes handcrafts and produce to sell at Portsmouth Market, purchases supplies, and returns home to begin the cycle again. The simply written text is complemented by full-color illustrations executed in a style reminiscent of American primitive painting. A Caldecott Medal Book.

Hoban, Russell. **Bedtime for Frances.** Illus. by Garth Williams. Harper. 1960. 32p. $8.61; lib. ed., $9.89; paper, $2.95. Ages 3–5.
Frances, a little badger, exhibits the familiar human characteristics of a child who at bedtime is determined to stay awake and finds innumerable excuses for attention. Pleasing sequels, illustrated by Lillian Hoban, include **Bread and Jam for Frances, A Baby Sister for Frances**, and **A Birthday for Frances**.

Hoban, Tana. **Count and See.** Photos by the author. Macmillan. 1972. unp. $10.95; paper, $2.25. Ages 4–7.

An uncluttered counting book in which photographs of articles familiar to small children reinforce the concept of numbers as words, numerals, and objects. Hoban's other creative photo books for the very young include **Look Again!** and **A.B.See!**

Hurd, Edith Thatcher. **I Dance in My Red Pajamas.** Illus. by Emily Arnold McCully. Harper. 1982. 32p. $9.89. Ages 3–5.

A warm and loving relationship is depicted between a young girl and her grandparents as they spend a "beautiful noisy day" filled with special secrets.

Isadora, Rachel. **Ben's Trumpet.** Illus. by the author. Greenwillow. 1979. 35p. $10.50. Ages 5–8.

Surrounded by bleakness, a young black boy dreams of becoming a jazz trumpeter. Stunning black-and-white graphics in an art deco style convey the 1920s setting. A Caldecott Honor Book.

Jonas, Ann. **When You Were a Baby.** Illus. by the author. Greenwillow. 1982. 24p. $10.25; lib. ed., $9.84. Ages 2–5.

Activities for babies to practice are cataloged in a presentation designed to boost the toddler's self-confidence. The author-artist's **Two Bear Cubs** is another story about early independence.

Kahl, Virginia. **The Duchess Bakes a Cake.** Illus. by the author. Scribner. 1955. 32p. $7.95; paper, $0.79. Ages 4–7.

The first in a popular series of rhymed picture books, this features the Duchess, whose 13 daughters are treated to a "lovely, light, luscious, delectable cake"—so light that it takes to the sky.

Keats, Ezra Jack. **The Snowy Day.** Illus. by the author. Viking. 1962. 32p. $10.95; paper, $3.50. Ages 3–6.

Full-color collage scenes depict a small black boy's joy as he plays in the snow. A Caldecott Medal Book. **Whistle for Willie**, which is illustrated in the same style, tells how a black child learns to whistle.

Knotts, Howard. **Great-Grandfather, the Baby and Me.** Illus. by the author. Atheneum. 1978. 30p. $6.95. Ages 6–8.

Upset by the arrival of a new baby, a boy gains understanding from his great-grandfather's recollection of how he and a friend rode many miles across the Canadian prairie just to see a new infant. Soft-pencil sketches match the story's gentle mood.

Kraus, Robert. **Whose Mouse Are You?** Illus. by Jose Aruego. Macmillan. 1970. unp. $9.95; paper, $2.25. Ages 5–7.

Both humor and poignancy distinguish a colorfully illustrated story about a mouse child who determines to find its missing family. **Owliver**, another engaging and funny picture book, tells of a young owl who resolves to make his own career choice.

Leaf, Munro. **The Story of Ferdinand.** Illus. by Robert Lawson. Viking. 1936. 64p. $10.95; paper, $3.50. Ages 5–8.

Lawson's expressive drawings expand the story of a peace-loving little bull who prefers smelling flowers to entering the bullring.

Lionni, Leo. **Frederick.** Illus. by the author. Pantheon. 1966. 30p. $6.99; paper, $2.95. Ages 4–6.

Frederick just sits and stores sunshine while five hard-working mice prepare for winter in a modern fable that parallels "The Grasshopper and the Ant." Inventive collages crafted from torn paper illustrate the story. A Caldecott Honor Book. **Swimmy** and **Inch by Inch**, also Caldecott Honor Books, are designed in a similarly inventive fashion.

Lobel, Arnold. **Fables.** Illus. by the author. Harper. 1980. 41p. $11.49; lib. ed., $11.89; paper, $4.76. Ages 8 and older.

This collection of 20 original fables features assorted animals who humorously exhibit human idiosyncrasies. Many of the maxims are modern and nontraditional; all are thought-provoking. A whimsical watercolor painting aptly illustrates each fable. A Caldecott Medal Book.

Lobel, Arnold. **On Market Street.** Illus. by Anita Lobel. Greenwillow. 1981. 34p. $11.25; lib. ed., $10.80. Ages 3–6.

A little boy shopping on Market Street sees stylish arrangements of an abundance of goods and groceries representing the letters of the alphabet. A Caldecott Honor Book. The same author-artist team created **How the Rooster Saved the Day.**

McCloskey, Robert. **Make Way for Ducklings.** Illus. by the author. Viking. 1941. 67p. $11.50; paper, $2.95. Ages 3–6.

Set in Boston Common, this enchanting picture book details a mother duck's determined efforts to take her brood on an outing in the park. Vitality permeates the sweeping illustrations. A Caldecott Medal Book. Other distinctive works by McCloskey include **Time of Wonder**, also a Caldecott Medal Book, and **Blueberries for Sal.**

Marshall, James. **George and Martha.** Illus. by the author. Houghton. 1972. 46p. $7.95; paper, $2.50. Ages 4–8.

Five separate adventures show that friendship is a deli-

11

cate matter, even with hippopotamuses. Both story and droll pictures have an appeal similar to that of the Babar stories.

Mayer, Mercer. **A Boy, a Dog and a Frog.** Illus. by the author. Dial. 1967. 32p. $8.95; lib. ed., $8.89; paper, $2.50. Ages 5–7.
    A hilariously funny wordless story about a boy and a dog who, though previously unsuccessful in their attempt to catch a frog, find the creature in their bathtub.

Musgrove, Margaret. **Ashanti to Zulu: African Traditions.** Illus. by Leo and Diane Dillon. Dial. 1976. unp. $11.95; lib. ed., $11.89; paper, $2.95. Ages 7–12.
    This ABC picture book based on customs and traditions of various African peoples is especially noteworthy for its art. A Caldecott Medal Book.

Provensen, Alice, and Martin Provensen. **A Peaceable Kingdom: The Shaker Abecedarius.** Illus. by the authors. Viking. 1978. 42p. $9.95; paper, $3.95. Ages 5–8.
    The illustrators have fashioned an animal alphabet drawn from the "Shaker Manifesto of 1882" into a charming and subtly humorous picture book. All the animals appear in pale hues on paper that has an antique look.

Rabe, Berniece. **The Balancing Girl.** Illus. by Lillian Hoban. Dutton. 1981. 32p. $10.25. Ages 5–7.
    Margaret, who is confined to a wheelchair, contributes to the school fair by creatively using her talent for balancing things. A warmly told story, illustrated in quiet tones.

Rey, Hans Augusto. **Curious George.** Illus. by the author. Houghton. 1941. 55p. $8.95; paper, $2.95. Ages 4–8.

12

George, a little monkey who is one of the most popular characters in American picture books, has one bad fault —an inexhaustible curiosity. In several amusing sequels, George perpetrates further innocent mischief. **Cecile G. and the Nine Monkeys** tells how a lonely giraffe befriends some homeless primates.

Rice, Eve. **Benny Bakes a Cake.** Illus. by the author. Greenwillow. 1981. 32p. $11.25; lib. ed., $10.80. Ages 3–5.
   A small boy and his mother spend the day baking and decorating a birthday cake only to discover that Ralph, the dog, has eaten it. A happy ending resolves this colorfully illustrated story. **Goodnight, Goodnight** is another simple picture book for the very young.

Rockwell, Anne. **Albert B. Cub and Zebra: An Alphabet Storybook.** Illus. by the author. Crowell. 1977. 32p. $10.53; lib. ed., $10.89. Ages 4–6.
   From Aa to Zz Albert B. Cub searches around the world for his missing pet zebra. Each lavishly painted watercolor is crammed with objects and activities beginning with the appropriate letter.

Rylant, Cynthia. **When I Was Young in the Mountains.** Illus. by Diane Goode. Dutton. 1982. 32p. $9.95. Ages 6-8.
   An Appalachian childhood is recalled in these reminiscences of family life in a mountain setting. Beautifully composed paintings in muted tones enhance the story's nostalgic mood. A Caldecott Honor Book.

Sendak, Maurice. **The Nutshell Library.** Illus. by the author. Harper. 1962. 4v. $8.95. Ages 3–6.
   Four miniature boxed volumes are humorously illustrated (each is also available in larger format): **Alligators All Around,** an alphabet book; **Chicken Soup with Rice,**

a book of rhymes; **One Was Johnny**, a counting book; and **Pierre**, a cautionary tale.

Sendak, Maurice. **Where the Wild Things Are.** Illus. by the author. Harper. 1963. 40p. $10.53; lib. ed., $10.89. Ages 4–8.

A childlike playfulness pervades this original fantasy about a little boy's adventures with deliciously grotesque monsters. A Caldecott Medal Book. **In the Night Kitchen** features bold illustrations that expand Micky's dream of an adventure in a baker's domain.

Seuss, Dr. **The 500 Hats of Bartholomew Cubbins.** Illus. by the author. Vanguard. 1938. unp. $6.95. Ages 5–7.

An amusing picture book tells of a boy who has multiple hats to take off before the king.

Sharmat, Marjorie. **Gila Monsters Meet You at the Airport.** Illus. by Byron Barton. Macmillan. 1980. 32p. $9.95. Ages 4–7.

Exaggerated reports of gila monsters "out West" make an eastern city boy apprehensive about his move to Arizona. Simple, colorful drawings depict the fears a child faces when moving to a new home.

Shulevitz, Uri, **Dawn.** Illus. by the author. Farrar. 1974. unp. $10.95. Ages 4–8.

A brief text accompanies luminous watercolor paintings that capture how the drama and beauty of night change to the fresh brilliance of a glorious sunrise.

Slobodkina, Esphyr. **Caps for Sale: A Tale of a Peddler, Some Monkeys and Their Monkey Business.** Illus. by the author. Addison. 1947. unp. $6.95; Scholastic, paper, $1.95. Ages 4–7.

A gaily pictured, popular tale about a cap peddler who

takes a nap under a tree full of clever monkeys. The story succeeds notably when shared with groups of small children.

Spier, Peter. **Noah's Ark.** Text by Jacob Revius. Doubleday. 1977. 42p. $9.95; paper, $3.95. Ages 3 and older.

Spirited illustrations picture Noah's well-known mission in amusing detail, highlighting the daily activities of the animals while they wait for the flood waters to recede. A Caldecott Medal Book.

Steig, William. **Doctor De Soto.** Illus. by the author. Farrar. 1982. 32p. $11.95. Ages 4–9.

Dr. De Soto, a mouse dentist, makes a nearly fatal error in judgment when he accepts an ailing fox as a new patient. Sprightly illustrations spark the story. A Newbery Honor Book.

Steig, William. **Sylvester and the Magic Pebble.** Illus. by the author. Windmill. 1969. unp. $4.95, paper. Ages 5–8.

Sadness comes to Sylvester's parents when the young donkey, a pebble-collector, accidentally turns himself into a stone. Large pictures in full color evoke the story's happiness, humor, grief, and final joy. A Caldecott Medal Book. Equally appealing works by this author-artist include **Roland the Minstrel Pig, Amos and Boris**, and **The Amazing Bone**.

Stevenson, James. **Howard.** Illus. by the author. Greenwillow. 1980. unp. $10.95; lib. ed., $10.51. Ages 5–8.

Pale watercolors over ink bolster a humorous text about a duck who misses the autumn migration and spends the winter in New York City.

Stevenson, James. **We Can't Sleep.** Illus. by the author. Greenwillow. 1982. 32p. $9.50; lib. ed., $8.59. Ages 4–8.

Louie and Mary Ann are unable to sleep, so Grandpa tells an outrageous tall tale of how he overcame the same problem years ago.

Thurber, James. **Many Moons.** Illus. by Louis Slobodkin. Harcourt. 1943. 47p. $8.95; paper, $3.95. Ages 6–9.

An original fairy tale of a princess who wanted the moon, and a court jester who got it for her. The soft watercolor illustrations add to the story. A Caldecott Medal Book.

Turkle, Brinton. **Deep in the Forest.** Illus. by the author. Dutton. 1976. unp. $9.95. Ages 4–7.

In an animated reversal of the "Goldilocks" tale, an impish bear cub tries the porridge, chairs, and beds he finds in a forest cottage. Lively three-color pictures tell the story in this wordless picture book.

Turkle, Brinton. **Rachel and Obadiah.** Illus. by the author. Dutton. 1978. 26p. $8.95. Ages 6–8.

Rachel proves girls are equal to boys when she wins a "tortoise-and-the-hare" race with her brother, Obadiah, and is the first to bring news of a ship's return. The Quaker ambience of the old Nantucket setting is as enticing as the lively story, the fourth in a series by this author.

Ungerer, Tomi. **Crictor.** Illus. by the author. Harper. 1958. 32p. $8.95; lib. ed., $9.89; paper, $3.13. Ages 6–9.

Crictor, the boa constrictor, adjusts nicely to life as a pet for Madame Bodot. Effective line drawings with green-and-red wash amplify the tongue-in-cheek humor and Gallic atmosphere. **Emile** and **The Three Robbers** are just as imaginative.

Van Allsburg, Chris. **The Garden of Abdul Gasazi.** Illus. by the author. Houghton. 1979. 31p. $11.95. Ages 5–9.

Strikingly meticulous, full-page pencil illustrations utilize light, shadow, and perspective to depict the exotic world Alan enters in search of his lost dog. Both the retired magician and his topiary garden prove too much for the boy, who returns home, pensive and confused, only to find the dog waiting for him. A Caldecott Honor Book.

Van Allsburg, Chris. **Jumanji.** Illus. by the author. Houghton. 1981. 32p. $11.95. Ages 5–10.

Finding an ordinary-looking board game under a tree, two children decide to take it home, only to discover that once begun, the game *must* be played to the finish. The fantasy is complemented by substantial full-page pencil drawings that offer fascinating perspectives. A Caldecott Medal Book.

Ward, Lynd. **The Biggest Bear.** Illus. by the author. Houghton. 1952. 84p. $8.95; paper, $2.50. Ages 6–9.

Strong black-and-white lithograph illustrations enliven an imaginative story of a boy who adopts a bear cub but later faces the heartbreak of giving the creature up when it grows to full size. A Caldecott Medal Book.

Wells, Rosemary. **Morris's Disappearing Bag: A Christmas Story.** Illus. by the author. Dial. 1975. unp. $9.95; lib. ed., $9.89; paper, $2.50. Ages 4–7.

Pastel drawings add charm to the tale of what happens when the youngest of four rabbit children is given a magic bag that enables him to disappear.

Wells, Rosemary. **Timothy Goes to School.** Illus. by the author. Dial. 1981. 32p. $7.50; lib. ed., $7.28; paper, $3.95. Ages 3–6.

The first days of school prove traumatic for Timothy, a rabbit, until he discovers a soul mate in Violet. Expressive faces and lively action add warmth. **Stanley and Rhoda** and **Benjamin and Tulip** are picture-book stories in a similar style.

Williams, Vera B. **A Chair for My Mother.** Illus. by the author. Greenwillow. 1982. 32p. $10.25; lib. ed., $9.84. Ages 4–8.

A little girl affectionately relates how her family saves coins to buy a comfortable chair for her mother to use at the end of her day's work. Brightly colored paintings with a folk-art motif add cozy tenderness. A Caldecott Honor Book.

Williams, Vera B. **Three Days on a River in a Red Canoe.** Illus. by the author. Greenwillow. 1981. 32p. $11.25; lib. ed., $10.80. Ages 5–9.

A child's diary of a family's canoe trip is full of fascinating detail, including recipes for outdoor cooking and instructions for knot tying. The illustrations have a childlike appearance, as if drawn in crayon.

Wittman, Sally. **A Special Trade.** Illus. by Karen Gundersheimer. Harper. 1978. 32p. $8.61; lib. ed., $8.89. Ages 4–6.

Old Bartholomew, young Nelly's special friend, is always doing things for her. When Bartholomew becomes confined to a wheelchair, Nelly has a chance to return the favors. A small book with tiny, expressive illustrations subtly promotes satisfying, positive relationships between young and old.

Yarbrough, Camille. **Cornrows.** Illus. by Carole Byard. Coward. 1979. 45p. $7.95; paper, $2.95. Ages 7–10.

As they practice the art of cornrowing on the heads of Sister and MeToo, Mama and Great-Grandmaw tell tales and sing songs from their African heritage. The large and lovely charcoal drawings are vital to the story.

Yashima, Taro. **Crow Boy.** Illus. by the author. Viking. 1955. 37p. $13.95; paper, $3.95. Ages 7–11.
The poignant, handsomely illustrated story of a shy Japanese child whose great gift is mimicking the sound of crows. **Umbrella** by the same author-artist was a Caldecott Honor Book.

Yorinks, Arthur. **Louis the Fish.** Illus. by Richard Egielski. Farrar. 1980. 32p. $10.95. Ages 5 and older.
"One day last spring, Louis, a butcher, turned into a fish." Louis seeks to change his life and, through appropriately bizarre watercolor illustrations and a brief text, the metamorphosis occurs.

Zelinsky, Paul. **The Maid and the Mouse and the Odd Shaped House.** Illus. by the author. Dodd. 1981. 27p. $9.95. Ages 3–8.
Adapted from an 1897 rhyme, this story depicts the creation of a house that has an unusual shape. Amusing line drawings brightened with color appear on rainbow-hued pages.

Zion, Gene. **Harry the Dirty Dog.** Illus. by Margaret Bloy Graham. Harper. 1956. 32p. $8.61; lib. ed., $9.89; paper, $2.95. Ages 4–7.
A picture-book favorite concerning a runaway dog whose increasing dirtiness prevents his being recognized at home. Equally entertaining sequels include **No Roses for Harry** and **Harry by the Sea.**

First Reading

Jaspersohn, William. **How the Forest Grew.** Illus. by Chuck Eckart. Greenwillow. 1980. 56p. $8.25; lib. ed., $7.92. Ages 7–9.

The growth of a New England hardwood forest on an abandoned farm over a period of two hundred years is deftly traced in poetic prose and pen-and-ink drawings. Questions for thought and discussion are included in this beginning reader.

Lobel, Arnold. **Frog and Toad Are Friends.** Illus. by the author. Harper. 1970. 64p. $7.64; lib. ed., $8.89; paper $2.95. Ages 6–7.

This first of several entertaining but simple I Can Read Books about Toad and Frog was named a Caldecott Honor Book for its lively drawings; a sequel, **Frog and Toad Together,** was voted a Newbery Honor Book for its writing. **Frog and Toad All Year** and **Days with Frog and Toad** show the companionable friends in other happy adventures.

Lobel, Arnold. **Uncle Elephant.** Illus. by the author. Harper. 1981. 64p. $7.64; lib. ed., $8.89. Ages 5–8.

When a little elephant's parents are lost at sea, Uncle Elephant moves in to care for him. Illustrations in soft tones reflect the warm and loving relationship that develops between the two.

Marshall, Edward. **Three by the Sea.** Illus. by James Marshall. Dial. 1981. 48p. $5.99; paper, $2.50. Ages 5–8.

Relaxing by the sea after their picnic lunch, three friends take turns telling their favorite stories. Comic illustrations highlight this book for beginning readers.

Minarik, Else H. **Little Bear.** Illus. by Maurice Sendak.

Harper. 1957. 63p. $7.64; lib. ed., $8.89; paper, $2.95. Ages 6–7.

The first of the publisher's I Can Read Books has charming three-color drawings that describe Little Bear's imaginative play adventures. A Caldecott Honor Book. Followed by **Father Bear Comes Home, Little Bear's Friend, Little Bear's Visit,** and **A Kiss for Little Bear.**

Parish, Peggy. **Dinosaur Time.** Illus. by Arnold Lobel. Harper. 1974. 30p. $7.64; lib. ed., $8.89; paper, $2.84. Ages 5–8.

Scientific information for the beginning reader is presented in a simple, amply illustrated, accurate text.

Sandin, Joan. **The Long Way to a New Land.** Illus. by the author. Harper. 1981. 64p. $7.64; lib. ed., $8.89. Ages 6–8.

Narrating the tale of his family's 1868–69 emigration from their Swedish farm to avoid starvation, Carl Erik tells of the hardships they endure and their fears, hopes, and dreams as they approach "The Golden Land" of America.

Schwartz, Alvin. **There Is a Carrot in My Ear and Other Noodle Tales.** Illus. by Karen Ann Weinhaus. Harper. 1982. 64p. $7.64; lib. ed., $8.89. Ages 5–8.

These stories about noodles, or silly people, are based on traditional Greek, Turkish, European, and American tales. Another easy-to-read book of folklore is the author's **Busy Buzzing Bumblebees and Other Tongue Twisters.**

Seuss, Dr. **The Cat in the Hat.** Illus. by the author. Random. 1957. 61p. $4.95; lib. ed., $5.99. Ages 4–6.

The first of the Beginner Books successfully combines a rhyming text and limited vocabulary with typically humorous Dr. Seuss drawings.

Shannon, George. **The Gang and Mrs. Higgins.** Illus. by Andrew Vines. Greenwillow. 1981. 48p. $8.25; lib. ed., $7.92. Ages 5–7.

A western Kansas trading post owner keeps her gold in an unusual but safe hiding place and thus out of the clutches of the nefarious Anderson brothers. Uncomplicated drawings capture the humor of this easy-to-read story.

Shaw, Evelyn. **Alligator.** Illus. by Frances Zweifel. Harper. 1972. 60p. $7.64; lib. ed., $8.89. Ages 6–8.

A science book for the beginning reader explores the habits of the alligator in an attractive I Can Read format.

Trier, Carola S. **Exercise: What It Is, What It Does.** Illus. by Tom Huffman. Greenwillow. 1982. 48p. $8.25; lib. ed., $7.92. Ages 6–9.

An introductory discussion of physical exercise is made interesting and accessible with perky, easy-to-read language and cartoon-like illustrations.

Van Leeuwen, Jean. **Tales of Oliver Pig.** Illus. by Arnold Lobel. Dial. 1979. 64p. $5.89; paper, $2.25. Ages 5-8.

Five delightful stories about the appealing Oliver Pig and his daily routines are successfully related in this multichapter book for beginning readers.

Folklore

Aardema, Verna. **Bringing the Rain to Kapiti Plain: A Nandi Tale.** Illus. by Beatriz Vidal. Dial. 1981. 32p. $9.95; lib. ed., $9.43; paper, $3.95. Ages 5–8.

With the plain dry and his cattle thirsty, Ki-Pat discovers a way to bring rain back to Kapiti Plain. This rhythmic, cumulative African tale with bright, full-color illustrations is well-suited for reading aloud.

Aardema, Verna. **Why Mosquitoes Buzz in People's Ears.** Illus. by Leo and Diane Dillon. Dial. 1975. unp. $11.95; paper, $2.50. Ages 5–8.

A repetitional African folklore is pictured in bold, stylized paintings that create a dramatic panorama for events set in motion by a mosquito's lie. A Caldecott Award Book. **Behind the Back of the Mountain, Black Folktales from Southern Africa,** and **Who's in Rabbit's House? A Masai Tale** are other African tales retold by Aardema and illustrated by the Dillons.

Bang, Molly. **Tye May and the Magic Brush.** Illus. by the reteller. Greenwillow. 1981. 55p. $8.25; lib. ed., $7.92. Ages 5–9.

Black-and-white drawings accented with red accompany this retelling of a Chinese tale about an artistic child who, in a dream, obtains a brush that brings to life everything she paints.

Bernstein, Margery, and Janet Kobrin. **The Summer Maker: An Ojibway Indian Myth.** Illus. by Anne Burgess. Scribner. 1977. 48p. $5.95. Ages 8–10.

A group of animals breaks into the sky and brings summer to earth. Large type and full-page, black-and-white drawings create an appealing book for younger readers.

Bierhorst, John. **A Cry from the Earth: Music of the North American Indians.** Four Winds. 1979. 113p. $12.95. Ages 11–13.

A fascinating study of the music of native Americans

includes many notes, sources, and bibliographies. Also available is a recording of the songs (Folkways FC 37777).

Billout, Guy. **Thunderbolt and Rainbow: A Look at Greek Mythology.** Illus. by the reteller. Prentice-Hall. 1981. 32p. $9.95. Ages 11 and older.

A remarkable and often humorous introduction to mythology offers modern interpretations of 13 myths, illustrated with bright, spare, posterlike scenes. Thoughtful readers will recognize the relationship between the familiar urban or technological panoramas and the ancient myth.

Blegvad, Erik. **The Three Little Pigs.** Illus. by the reteller. Atheneum. 1980. 32p. $9.95. Ages 3–5.

Faithful to Joseph Jacobs' original version of the well-known nursery tale, this small, carefully composed volume is full of detailed illustrations of animals in 19th-century costumes.

Brown, Marcia. **Once a Mouse: A Fable Cut in Wood.** Illus. by the reteller. Scribner. 1961. 32p. $12.95; paper, $2.95. Ages 5–7.

This old Indian fable about a hermit who transforms a mouse into a tiger sports handsome three-color woodcuts. A Caldecott Medal Book.

Brown, Marcia. **The Three Billy-Goats Gruff.** Illus. by the reteller. Harcourt. 1957. 32p. $10.95; paper, $2.95. Ages 3–6.

A simple Norse folktale about three goats that triumph over a cranky troll is dramatically enhanced by bold artwork.

Bryan, Ashley. **The Ox of the Wonderful Horns and Other African Folk Tales.** Illus. by the reteller. Atheneum. 1971. 41p. $8.95. Ages 6–9.

24

Four amusing stories of animal trickery are presented with a longer tale about a boy who solves his problems with the aid of a magic ox. Handsome black, red, and tan pictures in African folk motifs embellish this folklore collection, which reads easily.

The Cat on the Dovrefell: A Christmas Tale. Trans. from the Norse by Sir George Webbe Dasent. Illus. by Tomie de Paola. Putnam. 1979. 32p. $8.95; paper, $3.95. Ages 5–8.

Halvor gives up hope of ever being free of a band of greedy trolls until they mistake a great white bear for his new "cat." Full-page pictures feature grotesque but appealing trolls.

Chase, Richard. **Jack Tales.** Houghton. 1943. 201p. $10.95. Ages 9–12.

American versions of tales about Jack, that ubiquitous hero of folktales, who always emerges triumphant, either through quick wit or sheer good luck. **Grandfather Tales** was compiled by Chase from southern-mountain storytellers.

Coatsworth, Emerson, and David Coatsworth. **The Adventures of Nanabush: Ojibway Indian Stories.** Illus. by Francis Kagige. Atheneum. 1980. 85p. $10.95. Ages 9–12.

Full-color paintings rendered by an Ojibway artist illustrate 16 tales, collected from tribal members, about the trickster Nanabush.

Cooney, Barbara. **Chanticleer and the Fox.** Illus. by the reteller. Crowell. 1958. 31p. $9.57; lib. ed., $10.89; paper, $3.80. Ages 5–8.

A skillful adaptation of Chaucer's "Nun's Priest's Tale," in which the proud cock Chanticleer, betrayed by his vanity, is carried off by the sly fox but manages to save himself by his own wits. Striking designs and authentic medieval details make a handsome picture book. A Caldecott Medal Book.

Curtis, Edward S. **The Girl Who Married a Ghost and Other Tales from the North American Indian.** Ed. by John Bierhorst. Photos by the author. Four Winds. 1978. 115p. $10.95. Ages 10–13.

From Curtis's original 20-volume collection, Bierhorst has selected nine tales representing various regions of the North American continent, along with some of the original sepia photographs. The book is especially notable for its excellence in design.

D'Aulaire, Ingri, and Edgar Parin D'Aulaire. **D'Aulaires' Trolls.** Illus. by the retellers. Doubleday. 1972. 62p. $8.95; paper, $2.95. Ages 8–11.

Stone lithographs, in both black-and-white and full color, recreate the fantastic Norse folklore world of trolls.

Davis, Hubert. **A January Fog Will Freeze a Hog and Other Weather Folklore.** Illus. by John Wallner. Crown. 1977. 64p. $6.95. Ages 6–9.

Thirty short weather sayings of American origin, along with American variants of old-world weather lore, are set into double-page, black-and-white, finely detailed illustrations. Nine pages of notes explain the source of each saying and comment on its basis in fact or fancy.

Dayrell, Elphinstone. **Why the Sun and the Moon Live in the Sky: An African Folktale.** Illus. by Blair Lent. Houghton. 1968. 26p. $7.95; paper, $1.95. Ages 5–7.

From an early southern Nigerian collection, the brilliantly presented story tells of an invitation to Water and his subsequent visit to the home of the Sun and Moon.

26

de Paola, Tomie. **Strega Nona: An Old Tale.** Illus. by the reteller. Prentice-Hall. 1975. unp. $10.95; paper, $4.95. Ages 7–10.

A lively Italian variant of a familiar folkloric theme tells how a witch's helper nearly buries a town in pasta while tampering with her magic pot. A Caldecott Honor Book.

De Regniers, Beatrice Schenk. **Little Sister and the Month Brothers.** Illus. by Margot Tomes. Clarion. 1976. unp. $8.95. Ages 5–8.

A direct retelling, effectively illustrated, of an old Slavic tale in which a child is befriended by the 12 Month Brothers when her cruel stepmother orders her out into the snow to gather violets and strawberries.

De Roin, Nancy. **Jataka Tales.** Illus. by Ellen Lanyon. Houghton. 1975. 82p. $5.95. Ages 8–11.

Thirty ancient Indian fables from Buddhist lore have been retold authentically with their intrinsic humor intact.

Diamond, Donna. **Swan Lake.** Illus. by the reteller. Holiday. 1980. 32p. $9.95. Ages 7 and older.

Grey-toned, dramatic illustrations capture the magical enchantment of the ballet along with the tragic story of the beautiful swan and her unrequited love.

Emberley, Barbara. **The Story of Paul Bunyan.** Illus. by Ed Emberley. Prentice-Hall. 1963. unp. $4.95, paper. Ages 5–7.

Brown-and-blue woodcuts dramatically illustrate this simple but spiritual story of one of America's best-known folk heroes.

The Fox Went Out on a Chilly Night. Illus. by Peter Spier. Doubleday. 1961. 44p. $9.95. Ages 3–8.

The New England countryside provides the setting for an old folk song about the wily fox who raided the farmer's barn. Drawings in brilliant autumn colors alternate with sketches in black and white. The simple musical arrangement is by Burl Ives. Another folk rhyme illustrated by the artist is **London Bridge Is Falling Down.**

Galdone, Paul. **King of the Cats.** Illus. by the reteller. Clarion. 1980. 32p. $9.95. Ages 5–8.
   Using bold illustrations to set the tone of the story, Galdone retells the scary English folktale of the undertaker who sees nine black cats carrying a coffin and miaowing in unison.

Galdone, Paul. **The Little Red Hen.** Illus. by the reteller. Clarion. 1973. unp. $9.95; Scholastic, paper, $1.95. Ages 4–8.
   The familiar tale about the industrious hen and her three lazy companions is enhanced with spirited, colorful drawings that sprawl over double-page spreads.

Goble, Paul. **The Girl Who Loved Wild Horses.** Illus. by the author. Bradbury. 1978. 32p. $11.95. Ages 6–8.
   Action-filled, brightly colored paintings with contrasting black-and-brown shading illustrate the story of a native American girl whose overwhelming love of horses causes her to leave her people and go to live with the untamed creatures. A Caldecott Medal Book.

Grimm Brothers. **Snow White and the Seven Dwarfs.** Trans. by Randall Jarrell. Illus. by Nancy Ekholm Burkert. Farrar. 1972. unp. $8.95. Ages 6–9.
   The poet's excellent translation is complemented by full-page paintings which brilliantly recreate medieval settings. A Caldecott Honor Book.

Hodges, Margaret. **The Fire Bringer: A Paiute Indian Legend.** Illus. by Peter Parnall. Little. 1972. 31p. $6.95. Ages 7–10.

Adapted from a turn-of-the-century source, this tale shows how Coyote, the trickster hero, helped a young boy bring fire to his people. The vivid line drawings are highlighted with color.

Hogrogian, Nonny. **One Fine Day.** Illus. by the reteller. Macmillan. 1971. 32p. $10.95; paper, $2.95. Ages 4–7.

The repetitive action in this old Armenian tale shows a fox going from creature to creature and place to place to regain his tail, chopped off because of misbehavior. Beautifully designed illustrations are rendered in warm, rich colors. A Caldecott Medal Book.

Hyman, Trina Schart. **The Sleeping Beauty.** Illus. by the reteller. Little. 1979. 48p. $10.95; paper, $5.70. Ages 7–10.

The smooth retelling of the well-known story is expanded by detailed, full-color illustrations. From the elaborate christening scene to the ghoulish double-spread of the princes who died in the briar hedge, the artist successfully captures the fairy tale's drama and romance.

Jaquith, Priscilla. **Bo Rabbit Smart for True: Folktales from the Gullah.** Illus. by Ed Young. Philomel. 1981. 56p. $9.95; lib. ed., $9.99. Ages 7–10.

Bo Rabbit, an agile and clever animal, is the focus of an unusual collection of four folktales from the Gullah, Afro-Americans living off the coast of Georgia. Retold in modified dialect and illustrated with humorous, expressive black-and-white drawings in storyboard format.

Leach, Maria. **Whistle in the Graveyard: Folktales to Chill Your Bones.** Illus. by Ken Rinciari. Viking. 1974. 128p. $9.95; paper, $3.50. Ages 9–13.

Ghosts, witches, and other creatures that go haunting appear in short tales retold by a prominent American folklorist.

Lester, Julius. **The Knee-High Man and Other Tales.** Illus. by Ralph Pinto. Dial. 1972. 28p. $5.95; lib. ed., $5.47. Ages 8–10.
    From the rich tradition of black American folklore come six animal tales, illustrated in vibrant earth tones.

Lurie, Alison. **Clever Gretchen and Other Forgotten Folktales.** Illus. by Margot Tomes. Crowell. 1980. 113p. $8.61; lib. ed., $9.89. Ages 9–12.
    Fifteen short tales of aggressive, quick-witted young women are told in a readable, direct style with black-and-white pen sketches to add to the amusement. An introduction and source listing are useful for the adult storyteller.

McDermott, Gerald. **Arrow to the Sun: A Pueblo Indian Tale.** Illus. by the reteller. Viking. 1974. $10.95; paper, $3.95. Ages 5–9.
    Brilliant color and geometric figures invigorate a myth about a young Indian's search for his father, the sun. A Caldecott Medal Book. Illustrations featuring Ashanti tribal life form the basis for the author's **Anansi the Spider.**

Mayer, Marianna. **Beauty and the Beast.** Illus. by Mercer Mayer. Four Winds. 1978. 48p. $10.95. Ages 6–9.
    A satisfying retelling of the well-loved, many-faceted tale of a beautiful girl who releases a handsome prince from the spell that turned him into an ugly beast. Glowing, full-color paintings create a special world of beauty and romance in which all this seems credible.

Perrault, Charles. **Cinderella.** Illus. by Marcia Brown. Scribner. 1954. 32p. $11.95; paper, $2.95. Ages 5–8.

A strong fairy-tale atmosphere permeates the fluid lines and subtle colors of this romantic story. A Caldecott Medal Book. Other folktales freshly and individually interpreted by this artist are **Dick Whittington and His Cat** and **Stone Soup.**

Ransome, Arthur. **The Fool of the World and the Flying Ship.** Illus. by Uri Shulevitz. Farrar. 1968. unp. $10.95. Ages 5–9.

This Russian tale portrays a "fool" who wins the hand of the Czar's daughter with a clever ruse. Striking illustrations extend the folk motif. A Caldecott Medal Book.

Rockwell, Anne. **The Three Bears and Fifteen Other Stories.** Illus. by the reteller. Crowell. 1975. 117p. $10.95; lib. ed., $10.89. Ages 3–7.

Lively, humorous retellings of 16 popular nursery tales are matched in their simplicity by bright, cheerful illustrations. A companion volume, **The Old Woman and Her Pig and 10 Other Stories**, is styled in the same vein.

Schwartz, Alvin. **The Cat's Elbow and Other Secret Languages.** Illus. by Margot Zemach. Farrar. 1982. 82p. $9.95. Ages 7–13.

Descriptions of 14 secret languages and how they work use riddles and jokes to show hilarious codes from American folklore.

Schwartz, Alvin. **Scary Stories to Tell in the Dark.** Illus. by Stephen Gammell. Lippincott. 1981. 128p. $9.57; lib. ed., $9.89; paper, $4.95. Ages 10–14.

Well-known American folklorist Schwartz foraged through traditional and modern-day beliefs, legends, and ghost stories to concoct this delightfully ghoulish collection that has been given appropriately eerie illustrations.

Serwadda, W. Moses. **Songs and Stories from Uganda.**
Transcr. and ed. by Hewitt Pantaleoni. Illus. by Leo and
Diane Dillon. Crowell. 1974. 80p. $9.57; lib. ed., $9.89.
Ages 7–10.

Musical notation for singing and drumming these translated African songs and stories make this a novel storytelling volume, embellished with striking woodcut illustrations.

Shannon, George. **The Piney Woods Peddler.** Illus. by
Nancy Tafuri. Greenwillow. 1981. 32p. $10.25; lib. ed.,
$9.84. Ages 3–6.

An amiable peddler will swap or trade almost anything
to get a shiny silver dollar for his "dear darling daughter."
A lilting refrain links episodes pictured in bright, boldly
shaped paintings in this version of a tale also known as
"The Twice Bitten Stick."

Shulevitz, Uri. **The Treasure.** Illus. by the reteller. Farrar.
1979. 31p. $8.95. Ages 5–9.

Brilliant, jewel-toned illustrations enrich this traditional eastern European folktale, in which Isaac travels to
the capital in search of a treasure revealed to him in a
dream. A Caldecott Honor Book.

Singer, Isaac Bashevis. **Zlateh the Goat and Other Stories.**
Illus. by Maurice Sendak. Harper. 1966. 90p. $12.95; lib.
ed., $12.89. All ages.

A choice volume of seven Jewish tales from eastern
Europe, superbly told and illustrated. Another collection
by this famous storyteller is **When Shlemiel Went to War-
saw and Other Stories**, illustrated by Margot Zemach.

Sleator, William. **The Angry Moon.** Illus. by Blair Lent.
Atlantic. 1970. 45p. $4.95. Ages 5–8.

Based on an Alaskan Indian legend and illustrated in

glowing full-color paintings that are elaborations on original Tlingit motifs, this tale relates a boy's rescue of his friend, held prisoner by the moon because she laughed at its ugly face. A Caldecott Honor Book.

The Talking Stone: An Anthology of Native American Tales and Legends. Ed. by Dorothy de Wit. Illus. by Donald Crews. Greenwillow. 1979. 213p. $11.95; lib. ed., $11.47. Ages 10–13.

Carefully collected and retold stories of creation, tribal heroes, and tricksters are arranged in groups by broad geographic regions and identified as to tribal origin. Brief notes and source information are provided, and black-and-white graphics, suggestive of native American motifs, complement the stories.

Towle, Faith M., **The Magic Cooking Pot: A Folktale of India.** Illus. by the reteller. Houghton. 1975. 40p. $6.95. Ages 5–8.

Batik designs in rich natural colors enhance a simply told tale of the magic pot that is stolen but eventually restored to its rightful owner.

Tresselt, Alvin. **The Mitten.** Illus. by Yaroslava. Lothrop. 1964. unp. $10.80. Ages 5–8.

A little boy's mitten, lost in the snow, becomes a haven for small animals in this retelling of an old Ukrainian folktale.

The Whistling Skeleton: American Indian Tales of the Supernatural. Collected by George Bird Grinnell. Ed. by John Bierhorst. Illus. by Robert Andrew Parker. Four Winds. 1982. 128p. $12.95. Ages 7–11.

Authentic examples of native storytelling collected in the late nineteenth century include mystery stories, dreams, and omens that foretell the future.

Wolkstein, Diane. **The Magic Orange Tree, and Other Haitian Folktales.** Illus. by Elsa Henriquez. Schocken. 1978. 212p. $5.95, paper. Ages 11–14.

Twenty-seven somewhat mature stories recorded during public storytelling sessions in Haiti have been carefully transcribed and edited with detailed source information appended. The tales are lively and offer a rare opportunity to share in a living folk art.

Womenfolk and Fairy Tales. Ed. by Rosemary Minard. Houghton. 1975. 176p. $6.95. Ages 9–12.

Drawing on folklore from around the world, Minard collects stories that portray women as strong, clever, and faithful characters.

Zemach, Harve. **Duffy and the Devil: A Cornish Tale.** Ilus. by Margot Zemach. Farrar. 1973. unp. $10.95. Ages 5–8.

A Cornish variant of "Rumpelstiltskin" features distinctive, droll pictures painted in harmonious colors. A Caldecott Medal Book. **The Judge** is another entertaining tale by the same reteller-artist team.

Zemach, Margot. **It Could Always Be Worse: A Yiddish Folktale.** Illus. by the reteller. Farrar. 1977. 32p. $10.95; Scholastic, paper, $1.95. Ages 5–8.

A man consults a rabbi for relief from the constant crying of his six children and frequent quarrels with his wife, but the solution is far worse than the original situation. Exuberant paintings in earthy tones add to the story's fine sense of the ridiculous. A Caldecott Honor Book.

34

Fiction

Alexander, Lloyd. **The Book of Three.** Holt. 1964. 217p. $9.70; Dell, paper, $2.25. Ages 9–12.

Inspired by ancient Welsh legends, the author has created Prydain, a mythical land of kings and villains, in which Taran, an Assistant Pig-Keeper, becomes a hero. Four sequels include **The Black Cauldron, The Castle of Llyr, Taran Wanderer,** and **The High King**, the last a Newbery Medal Book.

Alexander, Lloyd. **Westmark.** Dutton. 1981. 184p. $10.95; Dell, paper, $2.25. Ages 11–14.

Fleeing the powerful Cabbaras, Theo is befriended by Count Las Bombas, a charlatan; his companion Musket, a dwarf; and Mickle, an unusual beggar girl. Together they travel to Westmark's palace where the king, grieving over the loss of his only child, allows Cabbaras to rule in his place. Followed by **The Kestrel**, in which the country of Westmark is torn by war.

Ames, Mildred. **Anna to the Infinite Power.** Scribner. 1981. 198p. $11.95; Scholastic, paper, $1.95. Ages 11–14.

A 12-year-old math genius living in the 1990s, who seems to be a human computer, accidentally learns she is a clone involved in an experiment with sinister overtones.

Armstrong, William H. **Sounder.** Harper. 1969. 116p. $8.95; lib. ed., $9.89; paper, $2.50. Ages 12–15.

The shattering experiences of a black sharecropper's family—the father's severe sentence for the theft of food and the maiming of the great dog Sounder—are related in a poignant novel. A Newbery Medal Book.

Babbitt, Natalie. **Tuck Everlasting.** Farrar. 1975. 139p. $8.95; Bantam, paper, $1.95. Ages 10 and older.

When the Tuck family discovers that a 10-year-old girl and a conniving stranger share their secret knowledge of a spring whose waters give eternal life, violence and profound questions about the implications of their immortality are the result. Other provocative tales by this masterful writer include **Knee-Knock Rise, The Devil's Storybook,** and **Eyes of the Amaryllis.**

Blos, Joan. **A Gathering of Days: A New England Girl's Journal, 1830–32.** Scribner, 1979. 144p. $10.95; paper, $2.95. Ages 11–14.

The quietly moving fictional journal of 13-year-old Catherine Hall tells of matters both large (a friend's death, adjustment to a stepmother, the slavery issue) and small in a memorable account of everyday life in early nineteenth-century New England. A Newbery Medal Book.

Blume, Judy. **Superfudge.** Dutton. 1980. 166p. $9.95; Dell, paper, $2.25. Ages 8–10.

Fudge, the younger brother in **Tales of a Fourth Grade Nothing**, is back. Here, boisterous, uninhibited Fudge and his older brother Peter cope with a new baby sister, moving to a new home, and entering a new school.

Bond, Nancy. **A String in the Harp.** Atheneum. 1976. 370p. $10.95. Ages 11–14.

Present-day Wales and the sixth-century fantasy world of Taliesin combine in this perceptive story of an American family's adjustment to the painful realities of a mother's death. **Country of Broken Stone** and **The Voyage Begun** are two other deeply moving novels by this insightful writer.

Bosse, Malcolm. **The 79 Squares.** Crowell. 1979. 187p. $9.57; lib. ed., $10.89. Ages 12–14.

A poignant tale describes the unlikely bond that grows between a teenager and an 82-year-old ex-convict. While exploring the old man's garden, Eric grows mentally and emotionally, developing new insights about himself and those around him.

Brenner, Barbara. **Wagon Wheels.** Illus. by Don Bolognese. Harper. 1978. 64p. $7.64; lib. ed., $8.89. Ages 6–8.

After a harsh winter spent in a Kansas prairie town, three black boys are left alone while their father seeks a better place to homestead. This fast-moving story of close family relationships and pride in self-reliance is set in the post–Civil War period.

Brink, Carol Ryrie. **Caddie Woodlawn.** Illus. by Trina Schart Hyman. Macmillan. 1973. 270p. $10.95. Ages 10–12.

In this biographical story of the Woodlawn family on the Wisconsin frontier in 1864, lively, red-headed Caddie and her six brothers and sisters have the courage to warn the Indians of an impending white man's attack on their village. A Newbery Medal Book.

Brittain, Bill. **The Devil's Donkey.** Illus. by Andrew Glass. Harper. 1981. 120p. $9.57; lib. ed., $9.89; paper, $2.84. Ages 8–11.

Dan'l Pitt is warned about Old Magda, the witch, but refuses to believe in magic until he is transformed into a flea-bitten donkey to be sold to the devil. Humor and suspense enliven this original folktale about a young boy and his clever rescuer, Stew Meat.

Burch, Robert. **Ida Early Comes over the Mountain.** Viking. 1980. 145p. $10.95; Avon, paper, $1.95. Ages 9–12.

Ida Early, a comical character who spins tall tales and dresses in overalls and clodhoppers, comes over the mountain to keep house for the Sutton family. When the children fail to defend her against their schoolmates' mockery, Ida leaves and does not return until the youngsters demonstrate their growth in sensitivity.

Byars, Betsy. **Summer of the Swans.** Illus. by Ted CoConis. Viking. 1970. 142p. $11.50. Ages 10–14.

This penetrating story tells of a 14-year-old girl whose concern for a retarded younger brother helps put her own adolescent problems in perspective. A Newbery Medal Book. Byars also demonstrates her ability for sensitive, realistic fiction in **The Midnight Fox, The Pinballs,** and **The Cartoonist.**

Cameron, Ann. **The Stories Julian Tells.** Illus. by Ann Strugnell. Pantheon. 1981. 71p. $7.95; lib. ed., $7.99. Ages 7–9.

Julian and his little brother Joey get into mischief with humorous results in six witty short stories. The accompanying line drawings depict a loving black family.

Cameron, Eleanor. **The Court of the Stone Children.** Dutton. 1973. 191p. $11.50. Ages 10–14.

In a thought-provoking time fantasy, an American girl of today and a French girl of another century meet in a San Francisco museum that was once a French chateau.

Cameron, Eleanor. **A Room Made of Windows.** Illus. by Trina Schart Hyman. Atlantic. 1971. 271p. $9.95. Ages 10–14.

A deftly written story features self-centered Julia, an aspiring writer, whose relationships with family and neighbors bring her greater maturity and understanding.

Childress, Alice. **Rainbow Jordan.** Coward. 1981. 142p. $9.95. Ages 11–14.

A strong, sensitive character study of black women, in which 14-year-old Rainbow, her 28-year-old mother, and her foster mother comment in alternating chapters on their lives and relationships with each other.

Clapp, Patricia. **Constance: A Story of Early Plymouth.** Lothrop. 1968. 255p. $10.32. Ages 12–14.
Realistic details of the life and loves of a pretty young girl in seventeenth-century Plymouth Colony flavor this substantial, lively chronicle.

Cleary, Beverly. **The Mouse and the Motorcycle.** Illus. by Louis Darling. Morrow. 1965. 158p. $9.50; lib. ed., $9.12; Dell, paper, $2.50. Ages 8–10.
Keith befriends a mouse named Ralph, whose mania for Keith's toy motorcycle leads to reckless adventure. Cleary makes splendid use of her ability for original make-believe both here and in the sequel, **Runaway Ralph.**

Cleary, Beverly. **Ramona and Her Father.** Illus. by Alan Tiegreen. Morrow. 1977. 192p. $9.50; lib. ed., $9.12. Ages 7–9.
The irresistible Ramona of **Beezus and Ramona** and **Ramona the Pest** tries to help her father cope with unemployment. Warmth and humor characterize a real child's-eye view of the world in this amusing tale and its companion, **Ramona and Her Mother.**

Cleaver, Vera, and Bill Cleaver. **Where the Lilies Bloom.** Lippincott. 1969. 174p. $10.95. Ages 10–13.
After her father's death, 14-year-old Mary Call Luther becomes the head of the family and works hard to gather and sell medicinal plants in a desperate attempt to keep her brothers and sisters together. A sharp, distinctive picture of southern mountain life. The Cleavers' **Trial**

Valley is also about the Luther family; **Queen of Hearts** features a different set of individualized characters.

Coatsworth, Elizabeth. **The Cat Who Went to Heaven.** Illus. by Lynd Ward. Macmillan. New ed. 1967. 62p. $9.95; paper, $3.95. Ages 9–12.

A poetic, legend-like story of a poor Japanese artist and his "good-luck" cat who watches him paint a picture commissioned for a Buddhist temple. Reillustrated by Ward, who did the pictures for the original 1930 edition. A Newbery Medal Book.

Cohen, Barbara. **Yussel's Prayer: A Yom Kippur Story.** Illus. by Michael Deraney. Lothrop. 1981. 32p. $10.25; lib. ed., Ages 6–9.

Reb Meir and his sons fidget and daydream through the Yom Kippur service while shepherd Yussel, left to care for the animals, prays in his own special way. Handsome sepia drawings capture the spirit of old-world Poland in this dignified retelling of a traditional Rabbinic tale.

Collier, James Lincoln, and Christopher Collier. **My Brother Sam Is Dead.** Four Winds. 1974. 216p. $9.95; Scholastic, paper, $2.25. Ages 12–14.

A dramatic and authoritative story of the American Revolution describes the agonies and injustices of the conflict as seen by the younger brother of a patriot soldier. A Newbery Honor Book.

Cooper, Susan. **The Dark Is Rising.** Illus. by Alan Cober. Atheneum. 1973. 216p. $10.95; paper, $2.95. Ages 12–14.

Will, the seventh son of a seventh son, learns that he is destined to play a dangerous role in combating the forces of the Dark. A Newbery Honor Book. The predecessor is **Over Sea, Under Stone; Greenwitch, The Grey**

King (a Newbery Medal Book), and **Silver on the Tree** complete this compelling, inventive series.

Cormier, Robert. **I Am the Cheese.** Pantheon. 1977. 234p. $11.95; paper, $6.95. Ages 12 and older.

A terrifying story, in which a family pays a deadly price to protect the government, is narrated by the child who stands alone, a victim and a prisoner of that "protection."

Cummings, Betty Sue. **Hew against the Grain.** Atheneum. 1977. 174p. $6.95. Ages 12–16.

When the Civil War erupts, 12-year-old Matilda Repass is jolted into the adult world when she witnesses the lynching of her brother-in-law, an event that changes her brothers and father forever. A few years later Matilda is brutally beaten and raped, and though she initially denies life and rejects all who love her, ultimately her determination to survive is restored.

Dalgliesh, Alice. **The Courage of Sarah Noble.** Illus. by Leonard Weisgard. Scribner. 1954. 52p. $6.95; paper, $5.95. Ages 8–10.

This simply told story, based on a true incident, relates the experiences of a pioneer child whose courage is severely tested when she and her father settle in the Indian-inhabited wilderness of Connecticut. A Newbery Honor Book.

DeJong, Meindert. **The House of Sixty Fathers.** Illus. by Maurice Sendak. Harper. 1956. 189p. $10.89. Ages 10–12.

During the bombing of his country in World War II, a Chinese boy makes his way to safety with the help of 60 American aviators in this poignant and compelling novel. DeJong, a Hans Christian Andersen medalist, is also the author of **The Wheel on the School**, a Newbery Medal Book.

Du Bois, William Pène. **The Twenty-one Balloons.** Illus. by the author. Viking. 1947. 179p. $9.95; Dell, paper, $2.25. Ages 10–13.

Wonderful illustrations accompany the hilarious adventures of Professor Sherman, whose three-week flight in a giant balloon includes a stopover on the erupting island of Krakatoa.

Eager, Edward. **Half Magic.** Illus. by N. M. Bodecker. Harcourt. 1954. 217p. $8.95; paper, $3.95. Ages 8–12.

A family of imaginative children discover a magic coin that grants half-wishes, transporting them to other times and places—though not always in the way they expected.

Estes, Eleanor. **The Hundred Dresses.** Illus. by Louis Slobodkin. Harcourt. 1944. 80p. $8.95; paper, $3.95. Ages 9–12.

In this unforgettable story, underprivileged Wanda Petronski always wears the same clean, faded dress to school but invents "a hundred dresses"—on paper—for her teasing schoolmates. Other engaging works by Estes include **The Moffats, The Middle Moffat,** and **Rufus M.**

Fitzgerald, John D. **The Great Brain.** Illus. by Mercer Mayer. Dial. 1967. 165p. $9.95; lib. ed., $9.89; Dell, paper, $2.50. Ages 10–12.

John, the narrator, recalls the escapades of his older brother Tom, who is known for his crafty schemes. A witty, warm story with a turn-of-the-century setting.

Fitzhugh, Louise. **Harriet the Spy.** Illus. by the author. Harper. 1964. 289p. $10.53; lib. ed., $10.89; Dell, paper, $1.75. Ages 9–12.

A precocious New York City child keeps a diary in which she records penetrating and sometimes unwelcome truths about her schoolmates and the adults in her life.

Harriet's uninhibited behavior and the story's robust humor make this a favorite with children.

Fleischman, Sid. **Humbug Mountain.** Illus. by Eric von Schmidt. Atlantic. 1978. 149p. $8.95; Scholastic, paper, $1.75. Ages 10–12.

Outlandish characters, preposterous situations, and piercing humor abound in this tall tale about the Flint family's adventures along the Missouri River during the frontier period. Fleischman's wry storytelling can also be sampled in **Mr. Mysterious and Company** and **The Ghost in the Noonday Sun.**

Forbes, Esther. **Johnny Tremain.** Illus. by Lynd Ward. Houghton. 1943. 256p. $8.95; paper, $2.95. Ages 12–14.

An injury to his hand ruins Johnny's dream of becoming a famous silversmith, but it turns him into a courier for the Boston Sons of Liberty at the beginning of the American Revolution. Historical facts and a vivid recreation of life in the 1770s are successfully integrated with Johnny's story. A Newbery Medal Book.

Fox, Paula. **The Slave Dancer.** Illus. by Eros Keith. Bradbury. 1973. 176p. $10.95. Ages 11–13.

The horrors of the slave trade are revealed through the story of 14-year-old Jessie, who is kidnapped and press-ganged aboard an America-to-Africa slave ship in the mid-1800s.

George, Jean Craighead. **Julie of the Wolves.** Illus. by John Schoenherr. Harper. 1972. 170p. $9.57; lib. ed., $10.89; paper, $1.95. Ages 11–14.

To escape from an arranged marriage, 13-year-old Julie flees her home and is befriended by wolves on the Alaskan tundra. The author's **My Side of the Mountain** is another strong story of survival.

Greene, Bette. **Summer of My German Soldier.** Dial. 1973. 230p. $9.95. Ages 10–14.

A Jewish girl living in a small Georgia town during the 1940s is mistreated because she befriends an escaped German prisoner of war. Another story with a southern setting features 11-year-old Beth in **Philip Hall Likes Me, I Reckon Maybe.**

Greene, Constance C. **Beat the Turtle Drum.** Illus. by Donna Diamond. Viking. 1976. 119p. $11.50; Dell, paper, $1.75. Ages 9–12.

Tragedy results when a horse-loving girl receives a birthday gift of a week's rental of a horse. Her accidental death and its impact on her family are movingly and perceptively portrayed. **Dotty's Suitcase**, a novel set during the Depression, also exhibits Greene's fine talents.

Hamilton, Virginia. **M. C. Higgins, the Great.** Macmillan. 1974. 278p. $9.95. Ages 12–14.

An exceptional, haunting novel describes a black boy's struggle to save his home and way of life in a coal-mining mountain community. A Newbery Medal Book. **Sweet Whispers, Brother Rush,** a time fantasy, is another expertly crafted novel by Hamilton.

Heide, Florence Parry. **The Shrinking of Treehorn.** Illus. by Edward Gorey. Holiday. 1971. unp. $8.95. Ages 7–10.

No one credits Treehorn's claim that he is shrinking, but a magical game alleviates the problem. Dry humor also permeates the sequel, **Treehorn's Treasure.**

Henry, Marguerite. **King of the Wind.** Illus. by Wesley Dennis. Rand McNally. 1948. 172p. $8.95; paper, $2.95. Ages 9–13.

Based on the history of the Godolphin Arabian horse that founded the thoroughbred strain of Man-o-War, this novel follows the adventures of a mute Arabian stable boy who journeys with the horse to England. A Newbery Medal Book. Another of this author's much-loved horse stories is **Misty of Chincoteague,** which describes the annual round-up of wild ponies on an island off Virginia.

Hinton, S. E. **Tex.** Delacorte. 1979. 194p. $10.95; paper, $2.25. Ages 12–15.

With their mother dead and their father off chasing rodeos, 17-year-old Mace, ready for college and a chance at independence, is left to care for Tex, a rambunctious 14-year-old. It is a tension-filled time for both as they fight to safeguard their futures.

Holman, Felice. **Slake's Limbo.** Scribner. 1974. 117p. $8.95; Dell, paper, $1.75. Ages 10–14.

Thirteen-year-old Slake, a victim of abuse and poverty, creates a refuge for himself in the subways of New York City in a superbly crafted survival novel.

Hoover, H. M. **The Delikon.** Viking. 1977. 148p. $9.95; Avon, paper, $1.50. Ages 12–14.

In this sophisticated science fiction tale, the author of the gripping Children of Morrow trilogy describes the revolution ending the long rule of Earth by the Delikon, an alien extraterrestrial race.

Howe, Deborah, and James Howe. **Bunnicula: A Rabbit Tale of Mystery.** Illus. by Alan Daniel. Atheneum. 1979. 98p. $9.95; Avon, paper, $1.95. Ages 8–10.

When vegetables start to turn white overnight, Chester, the family cat, suspects the new rabbit is actually a vampire. The story is drolly related by the family dog, Harold, who must contend with the overripe imagination of the histrionic Chester.

45

Hunt, Irene. **Across Five Aprils.** Follett. 1964. 223p. Ace, paper, $2.25. Ages 11–14.

An unforgettable story traces the impact of the Civil War on a midwestern family with divided loyalties; young Jethro must shoulder the burdens of the farm as well as the agony of brother fighting brother. A Newbery Honor Book.

Kerr, M. E. **Little Little.** Harper. 1981. 183p. $10.53; lib. ed., $10.89. Ages 12–15.

Alternating narratives from the viewpoints of two dwarfs, Little Little LaBelle and Sidney Cinnamon, provide the vehicle for an outrageous satire of contemporary middle-class mores in the United States which, astonishingly, avoids ridiculing the dwarfs whose feelings and aspirations are central to the novel.

Konigsburg, E. L. **From the Mixed-up Files of Mrs. Basil E. Frankweiler.** Illus. by the author. Atheneum. 1967. 162p. $8.95; paper, $2.95. Ages 8–11.

Running away with her younger brother because she feels unappreciated, Claudia chooses the Metropolitan Museum of Art in New York City as an elegant hiding place and ingeniously contrives to remain there for several days. A Newbery Medal Book. **Jennifer, Hecate, MacBeth, William McKinley and Me, Elizabeth** and **Throwing Shadows,** a collection of short stories, offer further proof of the author's wit and insightfulness.

Langton, Jane. **The Fledgling.** Harper. 1980. 182p. $9.57; lib. ed., $9.89; paper, $2.95. Ages 9–11.

Despite the rage of two unbelieving townspeople, Georgie determines to fly and, with the Prince of Geese, she does. Suspense and satire mark a fast-moving, highly original fantasy set in Concord, Massachusetts. A Newbery Honor Book.

46

Lawson, Robert. **Rabbit Hill.** Illus. by the author. Viking. 1944. 127p. $9.95; paper, $2.95. Ages 8–11.

When new residents move into the big house on the hill, the small meadow animals hope for the best in a fantasy rich in invention, characterization, and humor. A Newbery Medal Book. A sequel, **The Tough Winter**, is equally successful. The author-artist won a Caldecott Medal for **They Were Strong and Good.**

Le Guin, Ursula K. **Very Far Away from Anywhere Else.** Atheneum. 1976. 89p. $6.95. Ages 13 and older.

A brief but resonant novel about Owen, an intellectual, and Natalie, a serious musician, who wrestle with their personal integrities and romantic inclinations as they face advance studies in preparation for careers.

Le Guin, Ursula K. **A Wizard of Earthsea.** Illus. by Ruth Robbins. Parnassus. 1968. 205p. $10.95. Ages 11–14.

The haunting story of a quest made by Ged, an apprentice wizard, who is followed by a malevolent force in the strange world of Earthsea. Sequels include **The Tombs of Atuan**, a Newbery Honor Book that describes the underworld of tombs from which the high priestess Arha escapes, and **The Farthest Shore**, in which Ged, now an archmage, helps challenge the evil that threatens to destroy all wizardry.

L'Engle, Madeleine. **A Wrinkle in Time.** Farrar. 1962. 211p. $9.95; Dell, paper, $1.95. Ages 10–14.

Spellbinding science fantasy with allegorical overtones incorporates concepts of time travel, extrasensory perception, and supernatural beings. A Newbery Medal Book. The same characters appear in a compelling sequel, **A Swiftly Tilting Planet.**

Levoy, Myron. **Alan and Naomi.** Harper. 1977. 176p. $9.57; lib. ed., $10.89. Ages 10–13.

Alan, a New York City junior-high boy, befriends Naomi, a French girl who is so traumatized after witnessing her father's death at the hands of the Nazis that she cannot speak. Her fragile, new found confidence is shattered when Alan and a friend become involved in a street fight.

Lowry, Lois. **Anastasia Krupnik.** Illus. by Diane de Groat. Houghton. 1979. 160p. $6.95; Bantam, paper, $1.95. Ages 9–11.

Ten-year-old Anastasia, disgusted by the idea of a new baby in the family, reveals the complexities of growing up in her constantly shifting lists: "Things I hate" and "Things I love." **Anastasia Again** continues the story of this spirited protagonist.

Lowry, Lois. **A Summer to Die.** Illus. by Jenni Oliver. Houghton. 1977. 154p. $6.95; Bantam, paper, $1.95. Ages 10–13.

The twin mysteries of birth and death are perceptively interwoven in this novel of 13-year-old Meg, who watches her pretty and vivacious older sister succumb to leukemia. At the same time, Meg befriends a neighboring couple and witnesses the birth of their first baby. The author's **Autumn Street** is an evocative novel set during World War II.

McCaffrey, Anne. **Dragonsong.** Illus. by Laura Lydecker. Atheneum. 1976. 202p. $10.95. Ages 12–14.

Young Menolly runs away from her planet, Pern, because her father forbids her to create the music she loves in this finely crafted fantasy. Followed by a sequel **Dragonsinger.**

McCloskey, Robert. **Homer Price.** Viking. 1945. 149p. $10.95; paper, $2.50. Ages 9–13.

Homer Price, who belongs to the Tom Sawyer tradition of young boys and American humor, enjoys six adventures in a midwestern setting. Followed by **Centerburg Tales**, another collection of fresh and original episodes featuring Homer and his friends.

McKinley, Robin. **Beauty: A Retelling of the Story of Beauty and the Beast.** Harper. 1978. 245p. $10.89; lib. ed., $9.89. Ages 10–14.
In this expanded, embellished, and highly romantic novelization, Beauty tells her own story against a background of rich settings and well-developed characterizations.

Mathis, Sharon Bell. **The Hundred Penny Box.** Illus. by Leo and Diane Dillon. Viking. 1975. 47p. $10.95. Ages 7–10.
A moving story about the relationship between a 100-year-old great-great-aunt and her young nephew, who alone of his family understands why she cherishes an old box. A Newbery Honor Book.

Miles, Miska. **Annie and the Old One.** Illus. by Peter Parnall. Atlantic. 1971. 44p. $9.95. Ages 7–10.
A Navaho Indian girl believes she knows a way to prevent her beloved grandmother's impending death. The fine ink drawings are appropriate to the text. A Newbery Honor Book.

Monjo, F. N. **Letters to Horseface: Being the Story of Wolfgang Amadeus Mozart's Journey to Italy, 1769–1770, When He Was a Boy of Fourteen.** Illus. by Don Bolognese and Elaine Raphael. Viking. 1975. 91p. $10.95. Ages 10–12.
Through imaginary letters (based on primary sources) to his sister, "Horseface," the young prodigy reveals an extraordinary view of the eighteenth-century world of music.

Myers, Walter Dean. **The Young Landlords.** Viking. 1979.
197p. $11.50. Ages 12–15.

Members of a black teenage action group, Paul Williams and his friends unwittingly become landlords of a
neglected apartment building. Visions of easy money
quickly fade as they find managing the building a lot of
hard work. A well-conceived, humorous novel set in New
York City features likable characters and realistic situations.

North, Sterling. **Rascal, a Memoir of a Better Era.** Illus. by
John Schoenherr. Dutton. 1963. 189p. $9.95; Avon, pa-
per, $1.95. Ages 11 and older.

Looking back to his rural Wisconsin boyhood, the au-
thor recalls an idyllic and adventurous year spent with
Rascal, his mischievous pet raccoon. A Newbery Honor
Book.

O'Brien, Robert C. **Mrs. Frisby and the Rats of NIMH.**
Illus. by Zena Bernstein. Atheneum. 1971. 233p. $9.95;
Scholastic, paper, $1.95. Ages 8–12.

A widowed mother mouse, seeking help for her youngest child, finds a group of laboratory mice and rats (including her husband) that is being used by the National
Institute of Mental Health in this ingenious, credible,
and moving story. A Newbery Medal Book. O'Brien
also wrote the futuristic novel **Z for Zachariah,** about a
15-year-old who survives a nuclear holocaust.

O'Dell, Scott. **Island of the Blue Dolphins.** Houghton. 1960.
184p. $9.95. Ages 10 and older.

Karana, an Indian girl who survived for 18 years alone
on a California coastal island, tells the story of how she
created a life for herself. The author, a Hans Christian
Andersen medalist, produced a sequel, **Zia,** in which
Karana's 14-year-old niece plays a role in the rescue of

her aunt. Other tantalizing O'Dell offerings include **The Black Pearl, The King's Fifth, Sing Down the Moon,** and **Sarah Bishop.**

Oneal, Zibby. **The Language of Goldfish.** Viking. 1980. 179p. $11.50. Ages 12–14.

Thirteen-year-old Carrie fears a mental breakdown, and although she turns to her family for help, they try to convince her—and themselves—that everything is normal. Not until Carrie takes an overdose of sleeping pills does she get the aid she needs to accept the changes inherent in growing up. A riveting, perceptive novel.

Orgel, Doris. **The Devil in Vienna.** Dial. 1978. 256p. Dell, paper, $1.95. Ages 11–14.

Living in Vienna in 1938, a young Jewish girl and her close friend, daughter of a Nazi party member, are forbidden to see each other. But their friendship survives as they find ways to keep in touch while the world crumbles around them.

Paterson, Katherine. **Bridge to Terabithia.** Illus. by Donna Diamond. Crowell. 1977. 128p. $9.57; Avon, paper, $2.25. Ages 10–13.

Jess Aarons and newcomer Leslie Burke, fifth-grade schoolyard competitors, become best friends and share a secret, imaginary world. Natural dialogue, real characters, and a theme that affirms the joy of life even in times of tragedy are skillfully combined. A Newbery Award Book as is **Jacob Have I Loved. The Great Gilly Hopkins** is another fine example of Paterson's distinctive novels.

Paterson, Katherine. **The Master Puppeteer.** Illus. by Haru Wells. Crowell. 1976. 179p. $10.95; Avon, paper, $1.95. Ages 12–14.

In eighteenth-century Japan—a time of famine, violence, and the patterned world of the puppet theater—an apprentice to the famous Bunraku puppet troop becomes embroiled in the machinations of a Robin Hood–like brigand. **Of Nightingales That Weep** is another of the author's historical novels set in Japan.

Peck, Richard. **Father Figure: A Novel.** Viking. 1978. 224p. Signet, paper, $2.25. Ages 12–15.

Seventeen-year-old Jim Atwater, who has been a father figure to his younger brother since their parents' separation, exhibits marked antagonism when the two are sent to live with their father following their mother's suicide. In a tightly knit story of complex relationships, Peck conveys a unique understanding of today's youth.

Peck, Richard. **Ghosts I Have Been.** Viking. 1977. 214p. $11.50; Dell, paper, $2.50. Ages 10–13.

A spunky girl's "gift" for seeing specters triggers a number of happenings, including a ghostly trip back in time to the sinking *Titanic*. A sequel to **The Ghost Belonged to Me**, this occult comedy has just as much humor and adventure as its hilarious predecessor.

Pellowski, Anne. **Stairstep Farm: Anna Rose's Story.** Philomel. 1981. 176p. $9.95. Ages 10–12.

In episodes viewed through the eyes of five-year-old Anna Rose, warmth, love, and humor prevail on the Wisconsin farm of a large Polish-American family of 50 years ago. Forerunners to this are **First Farm in the Valley: Ann's Story** and **Winding Valley Farm: Annie's Story**.

Pinkwater, Daniel. **Lizard Music.** Dodd. 1976. 157p. $9.95. Ages 9–12.

A widely imaginative novel tells of a boy who thrives on late night television programs and begins to see lizards everywhere. **The Hoboken Chicken Emergency** is written in the same madcap vein.

Pope, Elizabeth Marie. **The Perilous Gard.** Illus. by Richard Cuffair. Houghton. 1974. 280p. $9.95. Ages 10–14.
A strong-willed young woman triumphs by rescuing the one she loves from the fairy folk in this skillfully woven historical fantasy set in Tudor England. A Newbery Honor Book.

Raskin, Ellen. **The Westing Game.** Dutton. 1978. 185p. $11; Avon, paper, $2.25. Ages 11–14.
An unlikely assortment of 16 people of different ages, backgrounds, and professions find themselves heirs to an eccentric millionaire's fortune. First, however, they must solve the puzzle outlined in the tycoon's will. Clever word clues allow readers to play the game, too. A Newbery Medal Book.

Rawlings, Marjorie Kinnan. **The Yearling.** Illus. by N. C. Wyeth. Scribner. 1938. 428p. $20; paper, $6.95. Ages 12 and older.
The drama of a boy's growing up in the lonely scrub country of Florida, his relationship with an understanding father, and the crisis of his deep love for a pet fawn are thoughtfully brought to life.

Reiss, Johanna. **The Upstairs Room.** Crowell. 1972. 196p. $10.95. Ages 10–14.
An understated narrative about the two-year confinement of a pair of Jewish sisters hidden by neighbors during the Nazi occupation of Holland. A Newbery Honor Book. **The Journey Back**, a sequel, finds Annie, the younger of the two, returning home to face unexpected problems of adjustment.

Robertson, Keith. **Henry Reed, Inc.** Illus. by Robert Mc-
Closkey, Viking. 1958. 239p. $10.95; Dell, paper, $1.75.
Ages 10–13.

Carrying out a summer assignment, Henry Reed has
an eventful time organizing projects to illustrate free
enterprise. Carried out with the help of the girl next
door, these diverting experiments are described as if recorded in Henry's own journal and illustrated with entertaining drawings. More of Henry's inventive fun is
found in sequels, including **Henry Reed's Baby-Sitting
Service** and **Henry Reed's Big Show.**

Rodgers, Mary. **Freaky Friday.** Harper. 1972. 145p. $9.89;
lib. ed., $8.79; paper, $1.95. Ages 10–14.

A hilarious story relates what happens when 10-year-
old Annabel finds herself turned into her mother—and
vice versa! **A Billion for Boris**, an equally fast-paced
urban comedy, describes how Boris, Annabel's friend,
uses a television that announces the next day's news to
change his mother's lifestyle.

Sargent, Sarah. **Weird Henry Berg.** Crown. 1980. 113p.
$8.95; Dell, paper, $1.75. Ages 9–11.

When a dragon named Vincent hatches from Henry's
100-year-old egg, Henry rallies to save him from scientific research and aids his return to Wales. A fast paced,
humorous, and touching fantasy by the author of **Secret
Lies.**

Sebestyen, Ouida. **Far from Home.** Atlantic. 1980. 204p.
$8.95; Dell, paper, $2.50. Ages 12–16.

After his mute mother's death, Salty takes his great-
grandmother to Tom, owner of the run-down boarding-
house where his mother had lived and worked. Grudg-
ingly Tom takes them in, and as they grow to respect and
care about each other, Salty finally guesses that Tom is

his father. **Words by Heart** is another acclaimed work by Sebestyen.

Selden, George. **Cricket in Times Square.** Illus. by Garth Williams. Farrar. 1960. 151p. $9.95; Dell, paper, $2.25. Ages 8–11.

Chester, a country cricket who is accidentally carried in a picnic basket to Times Square in New York City, becomes a musical sensation after he is befriended by a young boy, a mouse, and a cat.

Skurzynski, Gloria. **Manwolf.** Clarion. 1981. 177p. $9.95. Ages 12 and older.

When Danusha's son's teeth and urine turn red and his face and hands become scarred and covered with hair, the other serfs on the medieval Polish manor drive them away, fearing that the boy is a werewolf. The author's smoothly written novel **What Happened in Hamelin** is a retelling of the Pied Piper legend.

Slepian, Jan. **The Alfred Summer.** Macmillan. 1980. 119p. $8.95; Scholastic, paper, $1.95. Ages 11–13.

Living in Brooklyn, New York, in the 1930s, 14-year-old Lester, who has cerebral palsy, is a prisoner of his disability and his over-protective mother. At the beach he meets awkward but otherwise normal Myron, along with 12-year-old Alfred, who is crippled and mentally retarded. Joined by Claire, a witty, self-reliant girl who wants to be a sports star, the four build a boat for Myron and grow in confidence as a result.

Smith, Doris Buchanan. **A Taste of Blackberries.** Illus. by Charles Robinson. Crowell. 1973. 58p. $9.89; Scholastic, paper, $1.95. Ages 10–12.

When Jamie dies unexpectedly from a bee sting, his friends, who ran away from the swarming bees, struggle with their sorrow and guilt.

Snyder, Zilpha K. **The Egypt Game.** Illus. by Alton Raible. Atheneum. 1967. 215p. $9.95; paper, $2.95. Ages 10–15.

Resourceful, imaginative children of different ethnic backgrounds play the "Egypt game" after school following their discovery of a battered reproduction of the famous bust of Nefertiti. In **The Headless Cupid,** Amanda convinces her new stepbrothers and stepsisters to join her in "studying" the occult. Both are Newbery Honor Books.

Speare, Elizabeth G. **The Witch of Blackbird Pond.** Houghton. 1958. 249p. $10.95. Ages 10–14.

The colonial scene of Puritan Connecticut, where impulsive young Kit from sunny Barbados finds herself accused of witchcraft after befriending a lonely old woman, is vividly depicted. A Newbery Medal Book. Another gripping colonial story is **Calico Captive.**

Steig, William. **Abel's Island.** Illus. by the author. Farrar. 1976. 117p. $7.95; Bantam, paper, $1.95. Ages 7–10.

A Crusoe-like survival tale in which a gallant mouse is swept from his wife's side in a torrential storm and marooned on an island for a year. Two more cleverly illustrated, witty animal fantasies are **Dominic,** in which a dog hero fights the Doomsday Gang, and **The Real Thief,** concerning Gawain the goose, who is unfairly accused of theft.

Stevens, Carla. **Anna, Grandpa, and the Big Storm.** Illus. by Margot Tomes. Clarion. 1982. 48p. $7.95. Ages 8–10.

Anna and Grandpa, stranded on the Third Avenue El during the blizzard of 1888 in New York City, learn to understand each other more keenly.

Strete, Craig Kee. **When Grandfather Journeys into Winter.** Illus. by Hal Frenck. Greenwillow. 1979. 88p. $9.55. Ages 9–11.

Elderly Tayhua overexerts himself and dies while attempting to train a wild horse for his grandson, Little Thunder. A dramatic example of two recurring themes in U. S. children's books—the acceptance of death and relationships between generations.

Taylor, Mildred D. **Roll of Thunder, Hear My Cry.** Dial. 1976. 276p. $10.95. Ages 10–13.

A compelling story of a black family in the South of the 1930s starkly reveals their deprivations and struggles to hold on to their land. A Newbery Medal Book. The sequel, **Let the Circle Be Unbroken**, continues the narrative about the Logan family.

Voigt, Cynthia. **Dicey's Song.** Atheneum. 1982. 204p. $10.95. Ages 12–15.

Dicey learns about reaching out, love, and friendship as the Tillerman children settle in with Gram and her rural life-style. A Newbery Medal Book.

White, E. B. **Charlotte's Web.** Illus. by Garth Williams. Harper. 1952. 184p. $8.61; lib. ed., $8.89; paper, $2.50. Ages 8–12.

Now considered a classic, this farmyard fantasy immortalizes the unusual relationship between a spider, a pig, and a little girl who can understand animals. A Newbery Honor Book. Two other well-loved stories by this famous author are **Stuart Little** and **The Trumpet of the Swan.**

Wilder, Laura Ingalls. **Little House in the Big Woods.** Illus. by Garth Williams. Harper. New ed. 1953. 237p. $10.53; lib. ed., $10.89; paper, $2.95. Ages 8–12.

The first in the series of "Little House" books about Laura, her sisters, and Ma and Pa, this depicts the Ingalls' hard work, simple pleasures, and struggles to survive natural catastrophies, all lightened by family unity and love. Seven succeding volumes carry Laura to young adulthood. Six of the eight are Newbery Honor Books.

Wilkinson, Brenda. **Ludell and Willie.** Harper. 1977. 181p. $10.89; Bantam, paper, $1.75. Ages 12 and older.

In the sequel to **Ludell**, the protagonist and her childhood sweetheart, Willie, are about to graduate from a small Georgia high school and marry. Unforeseen events separate them, but their faith in each other is so strong that a happy ending seems assured.

Wiseman, David. **Jeremy Visick.** Houghton. 1981. 170p. $8.95. Ages 11–13.

A school assignment involving reading epitaphs in a local cemetery motivates Matthew to find out more about Jeremy Visick, who died in a mine disaster a century before. Drawn back into time, Matthew meets Jeremy and his family and is able, at last, to lay the lost boy's bones to rest.

Wojcieschowska, Maia. **Shadow of a Bull.** Illus. by Alvin Smith. Atheneum. 1964. 165p. $8.95. Ages 10–14.

Manolo, son of the great Juan Olivar, is torn between his village's expectation that he will follow his father in the bullring and his own secret passion to become a doctor. A moving, colorful story of Andalusian life. A Newbery Medal Book.

Yep, Laurence. **Dragonwings.** Harper. 1975. 248p. $10.89; paper, $2.95. Ages 10–14.

A sensitive perception of Chinese tradition permeates this absorbing and credible historical novel in which a young Chinese boy comes to California in the early 1900s to join his inventive father who dreams of designing aircraft. Two of the author's other novels that deftly probe the Chinese-American experience are **Child of the Owl** and **Sea Glass.**

Biography

Blegvad, Erik. **Self-portrait.** Illus. by the author, Harald Blegvad, and others. Addison. 1979. 32p. $8.95. Ages 9–12.

This whimsical autobiographical sketch of the internationally known illustrator Blegvad is filled with a variety of lively pictures, some by family members and friends.

Bober, Natalie. **A Restless Spirit: The Story of Robert Frost.** Atheneum. 1981. 224p. $10.95. Ages 12 and older.

A smoothly written, revealing biography of one of America's most revered poets.

Brenner, Barbara. **On the Frontier with Mr. Audubon.** Coward. 1977. 96p. $8.95. Ages 8–11.

A lively fictionalized diary, purportedly written by James Audubon's apprentice, chronicles the ornithologist's 18-month journey down the Ohio and Mississippi rivers and into Louisiana in search of natural specimens to study and draw.

Coolidge, Olivia. **Tom Paine, Revolutionary.** Scribner. 1969. 213p. $15. Ages 12 and older.

A thoroughly researched portrait of a man first hailed as a hero of the American Revolution and then rejected by those who had admired him.

Epstein, Samuel, and Beryl Epstein. **Dr. Beaumont and the Man with a Hole in His Stomach.** Illus. by Joseph Scrofani. Coward. 1978. 57p. $5.99. Ages 9–11.

After saving the life of a voyageur who received a gunshot wound in the stomach, Dr. William Beaumont made significant studies of human digestion by observing the hole in the man's stomach.

Epstein, Samuel, and Beryl Epstein. **She Never Looked Back: Margaret Mead in Samoa.** Illus. by Victor Juhasz. Coward. 1980. 64p. $6.99. Ages 8–12.

Having won a fellowship to study the Samoan culture, anthropologist Margaret Mead set off on a nine-month venture, resulting in her classic study, **Coming of Age in Samoa.** This biography for young readers is both factual and appealing.

Fritz, Jean. **Stonewall.** Illus. by Stephen Gammell. Putnam. 1979. 152p. $8.95. Ages 10–13.

An entertaining biography of brilliant but eccentric U.S. Civil War general Thomas Jackson, whose nickname derives from an epithet given him during the Battle of Manassas. **Traitor: The Case of Benedict Arnold** is another of Fritz's full-length, balanced contributions to the biography shelf.

Fritz, Jean. **What's the Big Idea, Ben Franklin?** Illus. by Margot Tomes. Coward. 1976. 46p. $4.95, paper. Ages 6–7.

An easily read, amusing account of the eighteenth-century printer, inventor, and statesman who played an influential role in colonial history. One of a series of brief sketches of American heroes including Christopher Columbus, Paul Revere, and Samuel Adams.

Greenfield, Eloise. **Mary McLeod Bethune.** Illus. by Jerry Pinkney. Crowell. 1977. 33p. $10.89. Ages 8–11.

A straightforward account relates events of the successful black educator's life, from her childhood struggle for an education in the post–Civil War South and founding of a college to her government service under Franklin D. Roosevelt. Soft-pencil drawings, help convey the flavor of Bethune's life and times.

Hamilton, Virginia. **W. E. B. Du Bois: A Biography.** Crowell. 1972. 218p. $10.53. Ages 10–14.
   A fully documented portrait of this black American leader-author-sociologist's successes and failures in his attempt to gain equality for his people.

Hautzig, Esther. **The Endless Steppe: Growing Up in Siberia.** Crowell. 1968. 243p. $10.95. Ages 11 and older.
   Directly and simply, Hautzig describes five arduous childhood years in Siberia during her family's enforced exile from Poland during World War II.

Morrison, Dorothy. **Ladies Were Not Expected: Abigail Scott Duniway and Women's Rights.** Atheneum. 1977. 139p. $6.95. Ages 10–14.
   A lively biography profiles a courageous Oregon crusader for women's rights who lived around the turn of the century.

Strait, Treva Adams. **The Price of Free Land.** Lippincott. 1979. 96p. $9.57. Ages 10–14.
   In 1914, when she was five years old, Strait's family homesteaded 160 acres of government-owned land in Nebraska. After three years of back-breaking labor, during which they lived in a sod house, the land became their own. Illustrated with photographs from the family album, this will be of special interest to readers of Laura Ingalls Wilder's **Little House** books.

Poetry

Adoff, Arnold. **All the Colors of the Race.** Illus. by John Steptoe. Lothrop. 1982. 56p. $10.25; lib. ed., $9.84. Ages 8–10.

Illustrated in brown-and-white tones, these expressive poems convey the richness of ethnic roots. A universality of feelings emerges from the free verse. **Outside/Inside Poems**, contrasting the world outside and inside the mind of a young baseball player, is by the same author.

Farber, Norma. **How Does It Feel to Be Old?** Illus. by Trina Schart Hyman. Dutton. 1979. 40p. $9.95. Ages 7–10.

Conversations between a grandmother and grand-daughter provide a stirring statement on aging. The poetic text is supported by graceful black-and-white and sepia illustrations, vividly juxtaposing memories of past and present. A fresh approach to an understanding of old age.

Frost, Robert. **Stopping by Woods on a Snowy Evening.** Illus. by Susan Jeffers. Dutton. 1978. 30p. $10.95. Ages 6–8.

Pen and pencil drawings washed with pale orange, blue, and green accentuate the soft, wintry double-page scenes accompanying each line of this well-known poem. Another wonder-inspiring introduction to Frost for young children is **You Come Too: Favorite Poems for Young Readers.**

Greenfield, Eloise. **Honey, I Love, and Other Love Poems.** Illus. by Diane and Leo Dillon. Crowell. 1978. 45p. $7.95; lib. ed., $8.89. Ages 6–8.

Sixteen poems express the love of a young black girl

toward family, friends, favorite places, and things. Charcoal sketches of the child, overlaid with scratchboard drawings made to look self-drawn, are essential to the mood and expression of the theme.

Jones, Hettie. **The Trees Stand Shining: Poetry of the North American Indians.** Illus. by Robert Andrew Parker. Dial. 1971. 32p. $7.95; lib. ed., $7.45; paper, $1.75. Ages 8 and older.
    Full-color paintings accompany these short prayers, lullabies, and war chants sung from one generation to another.

Kennedy, X. J., and Dorothy M. Kennedy. **Knock at a Star: A Child's Introduction to Poetry.** Illus. by Karen Ann Weinhaus. Little. 1982. 144p. $12.95. Ages 8–12.
    Over 150 selections are included in an anthology that illustrates the impact, style, and form of poetry. Pencil sketches enhance this book, which is especially useful for introducing poetry to children.

Moore, Clement C. **The Night before Christmas.** Illus. by Tomie de Paola. Holiday. 1980. 32p. $12.95; paper, $4.95. Ages 3 and older.
    De Paola's stunning illustrations set the traditional Christmas poem in a New Hampshire village. Striking, full-color paintings in the style of American folk art are surrounded by quilt-pattern borders throughout the book.

Pomerantz. Charlotte. **If I Had a Paka: Poems in Eleven Languages.** Illus. by Nancy Tafuri. Greenwillow. 1982. 32p. $10.25; lib. ed., $9.84. Ages 5–8.
    This collection of short poems in English uses words from 10 other languages including Yiddish, Serbo-Croation, and Vietnamese.

63

Prelutsky, Jack. **Nightmares: Poems to Trouble Your Sleep.** Illus. by Arnold Lobel. Greenwillow. 1976. 38p. $11.25; lib. ed., $10.80. Ages 9–11.

Rhythmic horror verses combine with scary pen-and-ink drawings to create a delightfully haunting book. The poet's **The Headless Horseman Rides Tonight: More Poems to Trouble Your Sleep** is a collection of similarly spine-tingling offerings.

Sandburg, Carl. **Rainbows Are Made: Poems by Carl Sandburg.** Selected by Lee Bennett Hopkins. Illus. by Fritz Eichenberg. Harcourt. 1982. 81p. $12.95. Ages 10 and older.

Themes of nature, the sea, night, everyday observations, people, and word play are found in this compilation of 70 poems, enhanced by bold word engravings. **Early Moon** and **Wind-Song** are other books of verse by this famous American poet.

Silverstein, Shel. **Where the Sidewalk Ends.** Illus. by the author. Harper. 1974. 176p. $12.45; lib. ed., $12.89. Ages 8 and older.

This potpourri of absurdly funny poems and drawings is immensely popular with both adults and children, as is another Silverstein collection, **A Light in the Attic.**

Willard, Nancy. **A Visit to William Blake's Inn: Poems for Innocent and Experienced Travelers.** Illus. by Alice and Martin Provensen. Harcourt. 1981. 45p. $11.95; paper, $5.95. Ages 7 and older.

Lyrical nonsense poems, inspired by the poetry of William Blake, combine with imaginative illustrations to capture the spirit of the inn's namesake. A Newbery Medal Book and a Caldecott Honor Book.

The Arts

Adkins, Jan. **Wooden Ship.** Illus. by the author. Houghton. 1978. 47p. $6.95. Ages 10–12.

The building of a fictional whaling ship of the 1870s is traced from the moment of her inception until she sinks 15 years later off the Bering Strait. Carefully labeled, step-by-step pencil-and-ink drawings reveal the crafts-manship of nineteenth-century shipbuilders.

Ancona, George. **Dancing Is.** Photos by the author. Dutton. 1981. 48p. $10.75. Ages 4–11.

"Dancing is a skip and a hop and a kick and a stomp and just feeling good," claims the text. Abundant black-and-white photographs expand this concept of dance with pictures of celebrations and entertainment from many parts of the world.

Arnosky, Jim. **Drawing from Nature.** Illus. by the author. Lothrop. 1982. 64p. $11.25. Ages 8 and older.

Guidelines for drawing scenery, plants, and wildlife become more than a "how to" exercise as Arnosky's comments and sketches help readers refine perceptions of nature's processes and their consequences.

Baylor, Byrd. **They Put on Masks.** Illus. by Jerry Ingram. Scribner. 1974. 46p. $7.95. Ages 8–10.

Poetic prose and colorful drawings based on Indian artifacts convey the significance of various masks that Indians and Eskimos construct from wood, skin, bones, and other natural materials for use in prayers and dances.

Children, Go Where I Send Thee. Illus. by Kathryn Shoe-maker. Winston. 1980. unp. $6.95, paper. All ages.

Full-color illustrations on midnight-blue backgrounds

capture the reverent tone of this traditional American spiritual. As each of the 12 verses is added, those preceding it are repeated. The musical arrangement is provided along with notes on the song's Biblical roots.

Cumming, Robert. **Just Look: A Book about Painting.** Scribner. 1980. 61p. $12.95. Ages 9–12.

In a brief, liberally illustrated text, Cumming explores the fundamentals of color, light, perspective, and mood through an examination of great paintings. He further heightens readers' understanding by explaining artistic principles and how they can be applied in reflecting on works of art.

Haddad, Helen R. **Potato Printing.** Illus. by the author. Crowell. 1981. 64p. $9.13; lib. ed., $9.89. Ages 8 and older.

Attractive potato prints accompanied by careful explanations of processes and step-by-step instructions are arranged in order of increasing difficulty. Useful as a primer or as a source of inspiration for the knowledgeable craftsperson or teacher.

Haldane, Suzanne. **Faces on Places: About Gargoyles and Other Stone Creatures.** Illus. with photographs. Viking. 1980. 40p. $11.50. Ages 10 and older.

Striking black-and-white photographs and a brief text introduce gargoyles and their history; many of the figures shown here adorn the National Cathedral in Washington, D.C.

I'm Going to Sing: Black American Spirituals. Vol. II. Selected and illus. by Ashley Bryan. Atheneum. 1982. 53p. $10.95. Ages 8–10.

Beautiful woodcuts depict movement in this collection of black American spirituals, which is a companion volume to **Walk Together Children.**

Krementz, Jill. **A Very Young Gymnast.** Photos. by the author. Knopf. 1978. 128p. $10.95. Ages 8–11.

The author-photographer documents a year in the life of a 10-year-old gymnast who one day hopes to be a member of the U.S. Olympic team. A similar approach is used in **A Very Young Rider.**

Lasky, Kathryn. **The Weaver's Gift.** Photos. by Christopher G. Knight. Warne. 1981. 58p. $8.95. Ages 9–12.

Beginning with the birth of a lamb, the reader is taken through the shearing, sorting, grading, cleaning, carding, spinning, and dyeing of wool to the weaving of a blanket. Black-and-white photographs picture the months of labor and its final reward.

Powers, Bill. **Behind the Scenes of a Broadway Musical.** Crown. 1982. 96p. $13.95. Ages 9–12.

The process of creating a musical from its conception to opening night is covered in this photographic essay, which describes the Broadway production of Maurice Sendak's "Really Rosie."

Rockwell, Anne. **Games (and How to Play Them).** Illus. by the author. Crowell. 1973. 43p. $8.61; lib. ed., $9.79. Ages 5–12.

Instructions for 43 indoor and outdoor games that require no equipment are cleverly illustrated by costumed animals drawn in full color.

Sandler, Martin W. **The Story of American Photography: An Illustrated History for Young People.** Little. 1979. 318p. $19.95. Ages 12 and older.

Outstanding examples of America's eminent photographers, from 1840 to the present, illustrate an extraordinarily readable history of a fascinating art form.

Schnurnberger, Lynn Edelman. **Kings, Queens, Knights and Jesters: Making Medieval Costumes.** Illus. by Alan Robert Slowe. Harper. 1978. 113p. $12.45; lib. ed., $12.89. Ages 10–13.

Photographs, diagrams, and lucid instructions delightfully demonstrate how to clothe an entire cast of medieval players using three basic costume shapes—the circle, the T, and the tunic.

Supree, Burton. **Bear's Heart: Scenes from the Life of a Cheyenne Artist of 100 Years Ago with Pictures by Himself.** Illus. by the author. Lippincott. 1977. 63p. $12.45. Ages 11–14.

Bear's Heart, a Cheyenne warrior and artist, was imprisoned in St. Augustine, Florida, in 1875, along with 71 other Indians accused of murdering a white settler family. While there, he kept a diary illustrated in colored pencils and inks. This facsimile edition includes a brief biography, and Jamake Highwater has appended an afterword explaining how Bear's Heart's drawings reflect his assimilation into the white culture and his subsequent, tragic abandonment of his own culture.

Walker, Barbara Muhs. **The Little House Cookbook.** Illus. by Garth Williams. Harper. 1979. 240p. $10; lib. ed., $10.89. Ages 9–14.

A cookbook based on Laura Ingalls Wilder's classic Little House series offers a fascinating look at nineteenth-century American cookery. While maintaining as much authenticity as possible, the recipes allow for modern measurements, kitchen equipment, and availability of ingredients. Included are appropriate episodes from the books and discussion of how foods were obtained and prepared during Laura's childhood.

Walker, Lester. **Carpentry for Children.** Overlook. 1982. 208p. $14.95. Ages 8–12.

Step-by-step directions carefully indicate how to build wood projects such as birdhouses and puppet theatres. Photographs and humorous drawings extend the text.

History, Peoples, and Places

Baylor, Byrd. **When Clay Sings.** Illus. by Tom Bahti. Scribner. 1972. unp. $2.95, paper. Ages 6–10.

The daily life and customs of southwest Indians are traced in a brief text accompanied by reproductions of pictures on ancient pottery fragments.

Bellville, Cheryl Walsh. **Round-up.** Carolrhoda. 1982. 32p. $8.95. Ages 6–12.

Black-and-white and color photos complement a brief text describing a spring cattle round-up on a South Dakota ranch.

Bernstein, Joanne E. **Dimitry: A Young Soviet Immigrant.** Photos. by Michael J. Bernstein. Clarion. 1981. 80p. $10.95. Ages 10–12.

The problems faced by a family of Russian Jews in adjusting to American life are given a balanced presentation in this up-to-date view of an increasingly common situation. The text is augmented with numerous black-and-white photos.

Demuth, Patricia. **Joel: Growing Up a Farm Man.** Photos. by Jack Demuth. Dodd. 1982. 96p. $12.95. Ages 11 and older.

The dedication and enthusiasm 13-year-old Joel feels for farming comes across clearly in a text that conveys great respect for a rural life-style.

Drucker, Malka. **Sukkot: A Time to Rejoice.** Illus. by Brom Hoban. Holiday. 1982. 96p. $10.95. Ages 10–14.

Historical background and descriptions of family customs fill out this account of the Jewish fall harvest festival, which includes crafts, recipes, and related activities. Drucker explores another Jewish holiday in **Passover: A Season of Freedom.**

Epstein, Samuel, and Beryl Epstein. **Kids in Court: The ACLU Defends Their Rights.** Four Winds. 1982. 240p. $9.95. Ages 12 and older.

Case histories give factual accounts of young people helped by the American Civil Liberties Union when they were denied civil rights guaranteed by the U.S. Constitution.

Fayerweather Street School Unit. **The Kid's Book of Divorce: by, for and about Kids.** Ed. by Eric Rofes. Greene. 1981. 123p. $9.95. Ages 10–14.

When books by adults failed to help them through their parents' divorces, 20 young people wrote this thoughtful handbook to provide the support, encouragement, and information they wished they had received.

Freedman, Russell. **Immigrant Kids.** Dutton. 1980. 72p. $11.95. Ages 9–12.

The lives and life-styles of children who immigrated to America between 1880 and 1920 are portrayed in period photographs and poignant comments.

Giblin, James Cross, and Dale Ferguson. **The Scarecrow Book.** Crown. 1980. 55p. $8.95. Ages 9 and older.

Fact and fiction—both historical and contemporary—combine to offer insight into cultural attitudes about the power of effigies. The well-researched account includes black-and-white photos, a bibliography, and instructions for creating a scarecrow. Two other intriguing works by Giblin are **The Skyscraper Book** and **Chimney Sweeps: Yesterday and Today.**

Greenfeld, Howard. **Passover.** Illus. by Elaine Grove. Holt. 1978. 32p. $6.95. Ages 7–11.
An attractively designed book with black-and-white illustrations describes the historical background of the holiday, the preparations for its celebration, and how the Seder is conducted.

Kherdian, David. **The Road from Home: The Story of an Armenian Childhood.** Greenwillow. 1979. 238p. $12.50; lib. ed., $11.96. Ages 11–16.
With great compassion the author chronicles the suffering of his mother and members of her family during the Turkish government's persecution of Armenians in the early 1900s. After years spent in terror and hardship, Veron Dumehjian, Kherdian's mother, came to the United States as a mail-order bride. A Newbery Honor Book.

Loeper, John. **By Hook and Ladder.** Atheneum. 1981. 96p. $7.95. Ages 10-12.
A fascinating look at the history of fire fighting in the United States emerges through anecdotal accounts, factual information, and well-chosen illustrations, including reproductions.

Macaulay, David. **Cathedral: The Story of Its Construction.** Illus. by the author. Houghton. 1973. 80p. $14.95; paper, $5.95. Ages 10 and older.
A brief text is expanded by meticulous drawings that show stages in the building of a Gothic cathedral from its inception in the year 1252 to completion in 1338. A Caldecott Honor Book. **Castle, Pyramid, Underground, Unbuilding,** and **City: A Story of Roman Planning and**

Construction are similar combinations of succinct text and breathtaking drawings by this author-artist.

Meltzer, Milton. **Never to Forget: The Jews of the Holocaust.** Harper. 1976. 217p. $10.95; lib. ed., $11.89. Ages 12 and older.

Riveting first-person accounts of experiences in World War II concentration camps and resistance movements are collected by an author who has written other fine books about people, problems, and causes, including **All Times, All Peoples: A World History of Slavery** and **The Hispanic Americans.**

Nance, John. **Lobo of the Tasaday: A Stone Age Boy Meets the Modern World.** Pantheon. 1982. 56p. $9.95; lib. ed., $9.99. Ages 9–11.

Photographs depict the life of Lobo, a boy of the small, primitive Tasaday tribe in a remote corner of a Philippine island.

Newton, James R. **Forest Log.** Illus. by Irene Brady. Crowell. 1980. 25p. $8.61; lib. ed., $8.89. Ages 7–9.

Charcoal drawings are carefully integrated with narrative to tell the story of a giant Douglas fir tree that supports plant and animal life for years after it falls **and dies.**

Pace, Mildred Mastin. **Wrapped for Eternity: The Story of the Egyptian Mummy.** Illus. by Tom Huffman. McGraw-Hill. 1974. 192p. $9.95; Dell, paper, $1.25. Ages 10–11.

A book of fascinating scholarship sheds light on the practice of mummification in ancient Egypt.

St. George, Judith. **The Brookyn Bridge: They Said It Couldn't Be Built.** Putnam. 1982. 128p. $10.95. Ages 11 and older.

Explanations of construction principles and contemporary photographs expand this intriguing narrative of the Roeblings' seemingly incredible feat—building a connecting span across New York's East River in the late 1800s.

Salvadori, Mario. **Building: The Fight against Gravity.** Atheneum. 1979. 192p. $10.95. Ages 12–14.
Principles of building and architecture are explained in understandable but thought-provoking terms.

Spier, Peter. **Tin Lizzie.** Illus. by the author. Doubleday. 1975. unp. $8.95; paper, $2.50. Ages 7 and older.
The artist's characteristic watercolor and ink-line pictures present a nostalgic panorama of American life from 1909 to the present, as Spier chronicles the experiences of various owners of a Model T Ford.

Tinkelman, Murray. **Rodeo: The Great American Sport.** Greenwillow. 1982. 64p. $9.84; paper, $7. Ages 10 and older.
Rodeo as a professional sport was derived from the work-a-day occupation of cattle ranching. Photographs depict bareback riding, calf roping, saddle-bronc riding, and team roping.

Tunis, Edwin. **Frontier Living.** Illus. by the author. Crowell. 1976. 160p. $16.95. Ages 10 and older.
A comprehensive text and meticulous illustrations convey the spirit as well as the practical details of pioneer living, beginning with the early eastern frontiers and stretching to the Far West of the United States. Succeeding attractive historical pictures of daily life, crafts, and implements are provided in **Colonial Living** and **The Young United States, 1783–1830.**

Weiss, Ann E. **God and Government: The Separation of Church and State.** Houghton. 1982. 132p. $8.95. Ages 10 and older.

Contemporary problems in the United States—abortion, censorship, and right-wing politics—are discussed in an objective and thoughtful narrative that focuses on applications of the constitutional principle of separation of religion and government.

Wolf, Bernard. **Anna's Silent World.** Lippincott. 1977. 48p. $12.45. Ages 8–11.
A sensitive photo-essay follows the daily life of a vivacious six-year-old who is profoundly deaf. Through the patience and encouragement of family and teachers she masters the ability to communicate, attends a regular school, and participates in many normal everyday activities.

Zerman, Melvyn B. **Beyond a Reasonable Doubt: Inside the American Jury System.** Crowell. 1981. 217p. $10.53; lib. ed., $10.89. Ages 12–14.
The strengths and weaknesses of the U.S. jury system are probed in a clear, straightforward manner. Both actual and fictional examples are used in explanations of jury selection and trial procedures.

Zisfein, Melvin B. **Flight: A Panorama of Aviation.** Illus. by Robert Andrew Parker. Pantheon. 1981. 119p. $17.99; $11.95, paper. All ages.
Watercolor paintings illuminate this history of flight, which begins with man's earliest theories and concludes with the supersonic transport.

Science and Nature

Aliki. **Digging Up Dinosaurs.** Illus. by the author. Crowell. 1981. 33p. $10.53; lib. ed., $10.89. Ages 6–8.

Detailed ink and watercolor drawings picture a trip to a natural history museum to see the dinosaur exhibit. A child, along with other spectators, provides information on the discovery of dinosaur bones, their identification, and reassemblage for displays.

Cole, Joanna. **A Cat's Body.** Photos. by Jerome Wexler. Morrow. 1982. 48p. $8.50; lib. ed., $7.63. Ages 7–10.

The behavior and anatomy of a house cat are explained in this photographic essay. Diagrams enhance the descriptions of this popular U.S. pet. Other outstanding books by the same team are **A Bird's Body, A Frog's Body,** and **A Horse's Body.**

de Paola, Tomie. **The Quicksand Book.** Illus. by the author. Holiday. 1977. 32p. $10.95. Ages 6–9.

A lecture on the hazards of quicksand, complete with colorful cartoon-style illustrations, is placidly delivered by a jungle boy as a girl slowly sinks to her shoulders in the slimy stuff. An original, humorous approach to informational reading.

Dowden, Anne Ophelia. **The Blossom on the Bough: A Book of Trees.** Illus. by the author. Crowell. 1975. 71p. $10.95. Ages 10 and older.

A botanical artist presents in essay form the primary characteristics of tree structure and reproduction, with exquisitely precise color paintings of leaves, flowers, berries, and nuts. **Look at a Flower** is delivered in the same painstaking style.

Grillone, Lisa, and Joseph Gennaro. **Small Worlds Close Up.** Crown. 1978. 64p. $8.95. Ages 10–14.

Two cellular biologists have photographed common objects such as chalk, feathers, snake fangs, and human hair through a scanning electron microscope. The startling results are juxtaposed with identifiable photographs of the same items. Detailed captions accompany each set of photographs.

Holmes, Anita. **Cactus: The All-American Plant.** Illus. by Joyce Ann Powzyk. Four Winds. 1982. 192p. $14.95. Ages 12 and older.

Information about the great variety of cacti native to the United States includes recipes, tips for home cultivation, and lists of places for observations.

Howe, James. **The Hospital Book.** Photos. by Mal Warshaw. Crown. 1981. 94p. $10.95; paper, $4.95. Ages 5–8.

This reassuring, straightforward treatment for the prospective young hospital patient introduces hospital personnel, equipment, texts, treatments, and procedures. The book is illustrated with a profusion of child-filled photographs.

Kohl, Judith, and Herbert Kohl. **The View from the Oak.** Illus. by Roger Bayless. Scribner. 1977. 128p. $12.95; paper, $4.95. Ages 10–14.

An unusual approach encourages better understanding of one's environment by studying how small creatures adjust to their world through their senses.

Lauber, Patricia. **Seeds: Pop, Stick, Glide.** Photos. by Jerome Wexler. Crown. 1981. 57p. $10.95. Ages 7 and older.

An impressive combination of photographs and text describes how animals, people, wind, and water carry seeds, in a presentation that fosters an appreciation of the plant world and all its wonders. **Journey to the Planets** is another remarkable photo-documentary.

Lerner, Carol. **Seasons of the Tallgrass Prairie.** Illus. by the author. Morrow. 1980. 48p. $9.75; lib. ed., $9.36. Ages 9–12.

The seasonal cycles that take place on an American prairie as well as changes resulting from fire and pioneer settlements are carefully described and illustrated with detailed black-and-white pen sketches. This is a factual, finely made book that implicitly conveys respect for the environment.

McNulty, Faith. **How to Dig a Hole to the Other Side of the World.** Illus. by Marc Simont. Harper. 1979. 32p. $10.89. Ages 4–7.

A young boy's imaginary 8,000-mile journey through the earth introduces a child to simple geological concepts. The colorful illustrations, vital to the text, offer an exciting visual experience.

Meyer, Carolyn, and Bernadine Larsen. **Eskimos: Growing Up in a Changing Culture.** Photos. by John McDonald. Atheneum. 1977. 215p. $8.95. Ages 12–16.

An insightful and highly readable account of the joys and frustrations of modern Eskimo life is presented through a look at the Koonuk family who live near the Bering Sea in Alaska.

Morrison, Velma. **Going on a Dig.** Dodd. 1981. 128p. $9.95. Ages 10–15.

Full of fascinating details, diagrams, and black-and-white photographs, this introduction to the world of archaeology describes a unique program that allows youngsters to participate in an actual dig and takes readers on a tour of a site yielding Native American artifacts from 5000 B.C.

Pringle, Laurence. **Death Is Natural.** Illus. with photographs. Four Winds. 1977. 54p. $7.95. Ages 9–12.

The inevitability and even desirability of death in the recycling process of the natural world are discussed in a dispassionate, objective style. Clear black-and-white photographs, a bibliography, and index contribute to this treatment of a difficult subject. Pringle's deep interest in ecology and living things is apparent in **What Shall We Do with the Land?, Frost Hollows and Other Microclimates**, and **Vampire Bats.**

Sattler, Helen Roney. **Dinosaurs of North America.** Illus. by Anthony Rao. Lothrop. 1981. 151p. $14.25. Ages 8 and older.
    Against a background of vast geological change, more than 80 kinds of dinosaurs are described in accurate detail and naturalistic drawings.

Simon, Hilda. **Snakes: The Facts and the Folklore.** Illus. by the author. Viking. 1973. 128p. $9.95. Ages 10–14.
    An absorbing discussion of many of the world's snakes, their characteristics and habits, is paired with meticulous illustrations that handsomely depict the reptiles' colors and patterns.

Simon, Seymour. **The Long View into Space.** Crown. 1979. 47p. $7.95. Ages 9–11.
    Eye-catching black-and-white photographs showing the earth, moon, planets, stars, and galaxies are accompanied by brief captions. **The Long Journey from Space**, concerning comets and meteors, is a worthwhile companion volume.

Wexler, Jerome. **Secrets of the Venus's Fly Trap.** Dodd. 1981. unp. $8.95. Ages 7–10.
    Strikingly magnified black-and-white photos illustrate the activities of this fascinating insectivorous plant, and several experiments are outlined for dramatic demonstrations of its feeding process.

Directory of Publishers

Ace Books
200 Madison Ave.
New York, N.Y. 10016

Addison-Wesley Publishing
Co., Inc.
Reading, Mass. 01867

Atheneum Publishers
597 Fifth Ave.
New York, N.Y. 10017

Atlantic Monthly Press
8 Arlington St.
Boston, Mass. 02116

Avon Books
1790 Broadway
New York, N.Y. 10019

Bantam Books, Inc.
666 Fifth Ave.
New York, N.Y. 10103

Bradbury Press Inc.
2 Overhill Rd.
Scarsdale, N.Y. 10583

Carolrhoda Books, Inc.
241 First Ave. N.
Minneapolis, Minn. 55401

Clarion Books
52 Vanderbilt Ave.
New York, N.Y. 10017

Coward, McCann & Geoghe-
gan, Inc.
51 Madison Ave.
New York, N.Y. 10010

Thomas Y. Crowell Co., Inc.
10 E. 53rd St.
New York, N.Y. 10022

Crown Publishers Inc.
1 Park Ave.
New York, N.Y. 10016

Delacorte Press
1 Dag Hammarskjold Plaza
245 E. 47th St.
New York, N.Y. 10017

Dell Books
  1 Dag Hammarskjold Plaza
  245 E. 47th St.
  New York, N.Y. 10017

Dial Books for Young Readers
  2 Park Ave.
  New York, N.Y. 10016

Dodd, Mead & Co.
  79 Madison Ave.
  New York, N.Y. 10016

Doubleday Publishing Co.
  245 Park Ave.
  New York, N.Y. 10017

E. P. Dutton, Inc.
  2 Park Ave.
  New York, N.Y. 10016

Farrar, Straus & Giroux, Inc.
  19 Union Square W.
  New York, N.Y. 10003

Four Winds Press
  730 Broadway
  New York, N.Y. 10003

David R. Godine Publisher
  Inc.
  306 Dartmouth St.
  Boston, Mass. 02116

The Stephen Greene Press
  Fessenden Rd.
  Brattleboro, Vermont 05301

Greenwillow Books
  105 Madison Ave.
  New York, N.Y. 10016

Harcourt Brace Jovanovich,
  Inc.
  1250 Sixth Ave.
  San Diego, Calif. 92101

Harper & Row, Publishers, Inc.
  10 E. 53rd St.
  New York, N.Y. 10022

Holiday House, Inc.
  18 E. 53rd St.
  New York, N.Y. 10022

Holt, Rinehart & Winston, Inc.
  521 Fifth Ave.
  New York, N.Y. 10175

Houghton Mifflin Co.
  2 Park St.
  Boston, Mass. 02107

Alfred A. Knopf, Inc.
  201 E. 50th St.
  New York, N.Y. 10022

J. B. Lippincott Co.
  10 E. 53rd St.
  New York, N.Y. 10022

Little, Brown & Co.
  34 Beacon St.
  Boston, Mass. 02106

Lothrop, Lee & Shepard Co.
  105 Madison Ave.
  New York, N.Y. 10016

McGraw-Hill Book Co.
　1221 Ave. of the Americas
　New York, N.Y. 10017

Macmillan Publishing Co.
　866 Third Ave.
　New York, N.Y. 10022

William Morrow & Co., Inc.
　105 Madison Ave.
　New York, N.Y. 10016

The Overlook Press
　12 W. 21st St.
　New York, N.Y. 10010

Pantheon Books
　201 E. 50th St.
　New York, N.Y. 10022

Parnassus Press
　4080 Halleck St.
　Emeryville, Calif. 94608

Philomel Books
　51 Madison Ave.
　New York, N.Y. 10010

Prentice-Hall, Inc.
　Englewood Cliffs, N.J. 07632

The Putnam Publishing Group
　200 Madison Ave.
　New York, N.Y. 10016

Rand McNally & Co.
　P.O. Box 7600
　Chicago, Ill. 60680

Scholastic Inc.
　730 Broadway
　New York, N.Y. 10003

Charles Scribner's Sons
　597 Fifth Ave.
　New York, N.Y. 10017

Sierra Club Books
　2034 Fillmore St.
　San Francisco, Calif. 94115

Vanguard Press, Inc.
　424 Madison Ave.
　New York, N.Y. 10017

The Viking Press
　40 W. 23rd St.
　New York, N.Y. 10010

Frederick Warne & Co., Inc.
　40 W. 23rd St.
　New York, N.Y. 10010

Windmill Books, Inc.
　201 Park Ave., S.
　New York, N.Y. 10010

Winston Press Inc.
　430 Oak Grove
　Minneapolis, Minn. 55403

Index

Compiled by Kristina Masiulis

Authors, illustrators, subjects of biographies, and titles are interfiled below.

98

Barbara Elleman is the children's books editor for *Booklist*, ALA's biweekly review publication of recommended books. She has worked as a children's librarian and is active in the Association for Library Service to Children. She frequently speaks on children's books and reading.

Composed by FM Typesetting Company
  in Linotype Palatino

Printed on 50-pound Glatfelter,
  a pH-neutral stock, and
  bound in 10-point Carolina
  cover stock by BookCrafters